I0416182

RITA

THE FOG

BY

LILA TANABE

This book is a work of fiction. Places, events, and situations in this story are purely fictional. Any resemblance to actual persons, living or dead, is coincidental.

© 2003 by Lila Tanabe. All rights reserved.

No part of this book may be reproduced, stored in a retrieval system, or transmitted by any means, electronic, mechanical, photocopying, recording, or otherwise, without written permission from the author.

ISBN: 1-4107-9803-8 (e-book)
ISBN: 1-4107-9802-X (Paperback)

This book is printed on acid free paper.

Portions of the proceeds from the sale of this book go to SCI Foundation for wildlife preservation.

1stBooks - rev. 07/30/04

CHAPTER 1

The fog had descended into London with a threat so fierce it caused the cancellations of most of the December holiday celebrations. Its tentacles, which sprouted endlessly at will, slipped easily into each and every existing crevice and grasped a solid hold on whatever lay beneath creating a solid root system for the immense cloud that enveloped the entire city and beyond.

Travel was severely limited and Londoners walked in slow motion as though they were making their way through a sticky, gray glue. Each step had to be carefully weighed. Shoes and clothing carried evidence of puddles that lie in wait to splash and stain. It was, therefore, possible for pedestrians, although not actually seeing their counterparts, to hear muddled voices expressing relief because they had missed a puddle or expressing gratitude for heavy boots. Of course, there were much louder profane comments when the atmosphere got the better of the situation.

"Never saw it this bad," mentioned George as he munched a snack while waiting for his lunch to be served. With the idleness of so many workers, the pub became a regular meeting place to spin yarns of former inclement times that had rendered people helpless. Many saw a glimmer of hope in their own futures at the bottom of a glass—or perhaps it was a fading of life itself they were seeing. Well, no matter. The pub was certainly the place to be.

George was not an expert on any subject having quit school in the third grade to help tend his ailing parents farm, but his charisma and caring personality was like a feast to hungry listeners.

His parents had named him George after the former King of England and had high hopes for him to accomplish a better life through education and meeting the right people. An outstanding student, George prepared to forge his way through school and into the more elite neighborhood. Then his father suffered the illness. It was an illness no one talked about because it was more of a curse. It had been Spring and George, although studious, still had plenty of energy to enjoy the outdoors with his classmates. They had been playing with an old canning jar with a chipped rim and George had slipped a stick into its wide mouth and flipped it over his shoulder. No one was more surprised than George when it became air born. They all stood and watched the incredible arc it formed as it floated through the air. George's father had just finished adjusting a stubborn piece of fencing and stood holding both hands on the small of his back to stretch when the glass rocket landed squarely on the nape of his neck. The glass, weakened with age and chips, shattered on impact and rendered its target helpless. He fell to the ground and the other children scattered in horror leaving George alone to deal with the tragedy.

George's father had been dazed but remained conscious so the two of them were able to walk into the house so he could rest and regain his strength. He received plenty of attentive care. A few days later they were all alarmed that the lump on the back of his neck still ached and had actually grown in size. A doctor was hastily summoned.

"There is nothing in medicine to help him...but he is so young and strong his body will no doubt fight it off," were the doctor's final words as he wrapped up his examination. There was something hollow about his voice.

George and his mother watched as the head of their family struggled with unrelenting weakness and slowly withered to a devastating death at Christmas time.

George promptly quit school, scaled back the farm and worked without ever even mentioning his father's illness. But every chance he got he read books and learned from his former classmates whom he could now only hope to chat with on occasion. Learning was in his blood; farming a mere way to eke out a living for him and his widowed mother.

Now as an adult, his mother long ago deceased, he remained on the farm with no desire to ever make it more than a meager living space. There was more spare time now though and he spent it at the pub.

So mesmerizing was George's tone that many patrons arrived early to await his appearance at the popular pub and as a result were a might tipsy when the huge wooden door swung open to reveal his muscular physique. With the sudden, albeit dim, light on his face coupled with a cloud of gray swirl behind him some of the more tipsy patrons were certain they had captured a glimpse into eternity. This aura, added to the soothing calm voice of his, often gave some quite a start. Later they would explain to their spouses and friends they had really been at the pub with their Savior. After all, they had seen him in the doorway.

Of late, however, George's captivating voice contained a hint of anxiety as though he had become more convinced than anyone of the certain doom of the future.

"It's an omen of the end of the world," George went on. "It's stated so. One thousand and nine hundred years will be here in less than three years and the end is nigh."

The year was 1897 and predictions abounded. The end of the Experience; the Last Judgment. And George was one of those convinced the world would soon harvest its own demise. Many of his listeners actually forgot their own lunches sitting in front of them with their appetites becoming insignificant while they pictured the rot and decay of the world. On occasion a few would pick at their food as though it was useless.

George continued his mesmerizing tone by quoting Reverend Baxter, "'the world will come to an end in 1901.'"

"The Devil himself is about town. Darwin's publication *Origin of the Species* has produced many evolutionary theories which cannot be disproved or explained," a worried voice offered.

Everyone agreed the Darwin publication was unsettling and a definite threat to their beliefs in Creationism.

"We are doomed!" was an oft-repeated phrase.

"And back in the 50's. Remember Lord Kelvin who studied thermodynamics and 'heat death'? To quote him, 'the earth must have been, and within a finite period to come, the earth must again be unfit for the habitation of man.'"

To further confirm the validity of the spreading pessimism was the Industrial Revolution. Millions of workers sweated in gloomy environments and created cities, which were considered too dangerous for even the hardiest person to venture out at night. The cities, already overflowing with people, were forced to accept millions more from farmlands that had yielded the poorest of harvests on record.

Some of the worst slums of England sprang up in London and became ravaged with disease on top of the despair. One-third of London's population was considered living in slums.

William Booth, the founder and first general of the Salvation Army compared the slums to Dante's Hell inferring man does not need images from a poet to see Hell; he only needs to walk our streets to see the horrors of the lost and the damned.

Others chimed in various conversations that they had no faith in civilization and were adamant about its future being lost to destruction in the near future.

Periodicals screamed in published articles about the decline and decay of Britain. Many articles predicted much insanity to roam the earth with accompanied suicides. After all, Jack the Ripper was still at large and his viciousness would threaten any normal person's sanity.

"Life itself will be history in less than three years...actually two years from now we will be experiencing our last Christmas Holiday," were George's last words for the day and the last thoughts of his audience as well.

CHAPTER 2

However dismal life was certain to become, some celebrations did continue as planned. Not everyone was in agreement with those who forecasted such bleakness and Rita Barnes was one of the most optimistic persons on earth. She was right now preparing for her own wedding.

"Mother, it feels as though a button has slipped loose. Please check it for me." Rita nervously pleaded as she turned her back to make the buttons on her wedding dress more accessible.

"Rita, I'm frightened." Said an equally nervous Mrs. Barnes.

After a pause and when the wayward button had been properly set in its place Mrs. Barnes continued, "The end of the world is so near. I don't like you going off to America. England...home is where you should be."

"Mother, I wish you would forget that nonsense. The world will not end anytime soon. Where do you get these inane ideas?"

"Well, your father heard George talking down at the pub. He is a wise man and knows a lot of important data to back his statements. Anyway others, too, are convinced our decadent society will shrivel and die. Why Lord Kelvin himself talked about 'heat death' and no one has seen it worse than it is right now."

"Mother, have you and daddy overlooked the writings of people who believe we are moving into a bright future? Why do you choose to ignore great people like Fredric Harrison who believes we are on the threshold of a great time; the age of great expectations and striving for better things." Rita continued, "I am so excited about John and I getting married. It was well worth the wait for us to both get our teaching certificates. With all of the scientific accomplishments of late and new ones on the horizon, we will perhaps create a spark in a fertile mind to generate even more advancements. That is our goal. Both of us together have emphasized and firmly agree on this issue. Further, you know how that wicked Queen Victoria thinks of women. It's a miracle I was able to accomplish a teaching certificate at all with her around. It is imperative we pursue our goal in America."

"Rita. Please!" Her mother implored. "Do not speak of the Queen in such a manner."

"Very well, Mother. How do I look?" asked Rita as she smoothed her pearl off white gown.

"Oh, such puffy short sleeves in December. You are sure to chill. And such a large stiff collar. Thankfully my grandmother's broach will hold the neckline secure and high enough to give some protection from the weather. The plainness of your skirt is perfect the way it leads the eye to the bottom of your dress which is so exquisite."

And exquisite was a most fitting description of it. Twelve inches above the hemline the delicate material was gathered, draped and tacked. Each succeeding point was gathered, draped and tacked exactly six inches from the previous point. Each tack was held in place by a small bow. Below these bows was a flurry of flowers and petals made of the same material so as to create a wonderfully three-dimensional effect. It all ended with a scalloped hemline, which was trimmed with individual pearls sewn along the very edge.

It was Rita who insisted on the pearls for she loved the luster and they afforded her a certain degree of comfort. Throughout her young eighteen years she had often gazed into her grandmother's pearls and lost herself to an enjoyable thought process that took her to no end of serenity. Only pearls were able to reach out to her and offer a dreamy scene of pleasant surroundings. For most of her life she had been saving pearls from Japan for this very occasion. Aside from her own pleadings for babysitting assignments and other odd jobs so she could afford to purchase every pearl she saw, Rita could expect to see loose pearls in her Christmas stocking every year and on her birthday. Yes, Rita Barnes had known her entire life what she wanted and she feared telling no one. Soon it was assumed that the definition of her life would be how she would live it.

"In other words, you look perfect, dear." said her mother in a shaky voice. Then she added, "But I will miss you so."

"You still have Gary at home for a few more years. I, of course, will miss you, Daddy and Gary terribly. Maybe you could set sail for America, too. John and I will always have room for you and you could even settle there if you wish. This gloomy place is doing nothing for you."

"Perhaps when Gary gets out of school. His life is now so intertwined with his friends and it was so kind of Mr. Rodgers to offer your father a job in his business. With unemployment so very high, we would be less than charitable to leave now. You are marrying well. The Rodgers' are kind people." Mrs. Barnes voice trailed off with a tinge of sadness.

Together as previously planned, they carefully stepped outside into the dense fog to walk the two blocks to the church. It would be safer in this weather. Mrs. Barnes carried her daughter's veil and train while warning Rita to pick up her dress and hold it above the damp walkway.

"Watch where you step, honey. And if you see someone lower your dress quickly so they won't think you are being risqué."

Rita giggled. "I can't even see my own feet in this fog. I say no one else will be able to notice us at all."

Rita was right. As they daintily stepped through the murky atmosphere they heard a familiar plodding of a horse and the creaking wheels of the carriage it was pulling; but they could not see either one. They could not even get the dimmest of glow from the church lights. They were thankful they could hear the peal of the bells from the church announcing to a seemingly lost neighborhood that a joyful wedding was about to take place.

Rita stepped daintily so as to miss a few puddles and where drops of moisture had accumulated and thus avoided too much soil on her white shoes.

"Oh, mother! This is the happiest day of my life! Listen to the beautiful sounds of the bells pealing from the church. They have never sounded so cheery."

"We once celebrated your arrival in that same church. Now it seems to be announcing to a waiting world that a couple with endless optimism will emerge with an enthusiasm which will have a most positive influence on the next century."

"It is so very important to John and me that we have your blessings and support, but we know you think our move to America a foolish act."

"You can always return to London. Count on our assistance for that, I tell you."

"Such moisture will destroy my hairstyle." Rita was trying to change the topic of conversation for nothing in the world would ever alter her belief in the new age and the value of teachers. She had toiled endlessly to achieve her goal of earning a teaching certificate and nothing would ever interfere with her future plans. She would marry John Rodgers today and together they would soon set sail for America, where they would settle and teach. They would forever be open to new ideas and adventures to help create a new world of thinkers as they entered the next century. Piffle on these idiots who condemn women and forecast gloom and doom. Nothing could intrude on her thoughts of a beautiful picture of their accomplishments for years to come. It belonged to John and her as a special loving but firmly secure tie.

They became silent as they traversed a muddy road, which required more attention to detail. There were dangerous ruts and the fog seemed to secure itself to their ankles and hide the hazards from their view.

When they stepped up on to the boarded walkway, Mrs. Barnes slipped but regained her balance quickly. The incident gave them both pause and they stood silently for a brief moment regaining their composure.

Suddenly Rita felt a stir of excitement throughout her body and exclaimed, "Look, Mother! We can see the lights from the church now. Even the fog, which seems to be multiplying, can't entirely hide the warmth of its glow."

Her excitement grew as they approached the church and when they entered through the large heavy wooden doors her heartbeat quickened even more as she caught sight of her father.

As they hugged she reminisced about her lifetime of feeling his warmth and love protecting her from all evils of the world. Rita became teary as some strange realization stirred inside of her. The feeling she would never again see her father crept over her, but it was promptly squelched. After all, she was to be married in a few minutes and had much to do yet. Besides, she was certain that all brides must experience the same feeling of rebirth into their own families.

Mrs. Barnes drew Rita's attention with extra combs and hairpieces to secure her now limpish curls. She piled them on top of Rita's head and adjusted the veil and train. When Rita added an ever so slight tilt of her head, they all realized they were gazing upon perfection. A quick dab with a damp clothe over her shoes and she was ready.

John awaited her at the altar as the music announced her stunning glide down the aisle on her father's arm.

But yet again that sinister feeling rose inside of her as though it could never be squelched. Something as nebulous as the fog was tearing at her insides.

It's silly. Ignore it. Rita told herself. *This is the happiest day of my life.*

CHAPTER 3

Except for one minor mishap the ceremony went smoothly and lovely. When John lifted Rita's veil a small ringlet, which had been attached to it quite suddenly fell and dangled over her right eye barely touching her eyebrow. Everyone thought it was a wonderful touch as though it had been planned to add to the gaiety of the occasion.

The weather, the dire predictions for the future and any gnawing feelings of unpleasant happenings had successfully been suppressed into a most unnoticeable spot.

It was a joyous occasion and the joy even accompanied them on the walk through the slimy gray fog to the reception that was held at the Barnes' flat.

It was roomy enough to accommodate all the people who had gathered to help celebrate the union. There were plenty of nourishments, not to mention the spirits, and an unusually large wedding cake. Rita and John each had a mother and two aunts who had worked tirelessly for weeks preparing the food and cake.

"How can I ever thank all of you for all this extra work," murmured Rita as she stepped into the kitchen. "All this warmth seems to be radiating from the food."

"You can thank us by living a long and happy life with John," offered one of her aunts.

"The food is meant to symbolize a warm and secure future," added her mother.

The theme of the meal was lobster. Three inch pastry shells contained Lobster Newberg. By the time a guest finished that delectable morsel, they were served Lobster Thermadore.

There was plenty of white wine of the lightest vintage and by the time the lobster shells were picked clean of the thermadore, a light Lobster Corn Salad made its way to the palates. No expense was spared for this glorious occasion for John's father had been quite successful with his own business over the years.

Rita's father, however, owned a business that was faltering; but not to worry. His daughter's father-in-law was waiting in the wings to offer him a new position that would actually be created just for Mr. Barnes. There was no animosity between them or clashes of egos. Quite the contrary; admiration and the utmost respect for each others efforts was obvious to anyone who knew them. But Mr. Barnes was determined to stick with his own business as long as possible giving it all the attention he could to insure, hopefully, a success soon to be passed on to his employees. He owed it to himself to diligently proceed with what seemed the impossible goal. He wanted one more time at it and he approached the awesome project with a most invigorating effort.

But, today, to enhance the celebration of the union of their offspring, food and drink was presented to all the men as they settled in the library of the Barnes' flat.

"Blimey!" Mr. Rodgers commented. "This fog seems to be multiplying itself into a most unseeming density. It has ceased even to swirl as we walk through it."

"Like an endless solid substance. It will last until the end of time," offered Mr. Carson, a neighbor.

"Oh, lets not start on the destruction of life and the world's so called leap into a vast wasteland."

"I think the kids made an excellent choice. They will be sailing for America in a few days, leaving all the devastation of London and headed for a new land," commented Mr. Barnes as he munched on a roll stuffed with cold lobster salad. The tasty treat went good with the warm brandy they had already opened and imbibed.

"It's good they have thought it out ahead of time. They actually have teaching assignments waiting for them. Sounds like a right good deal, too. New York is the center of many activities and the cultural aspects are quite attractive. It is astonishing they have actually been offered a home and a schoolhouse in such a booming area of the new world." Mr. Rodgers was obviously proud of his son and new daughter-in-law.

"And transport is always available for goods that must travel by water."

"Imagine! A house, a home for them, and a schoolhouse." Mr. Barnes was obviously proud also. "And they are planning a large family of their own."

"Excuse me." It was Rita's Aunt Emma stepping into the room. "I want to refresh your food. We'll be having cake before long so you gentlemen stay sober. And the newlyweds will be opening their gifts. Such as they are. There really are no practical gifts to give a couple floating away on a boat to a new land."

As Emma spoke she was replenishing the Lobster Fettuccine and the gentlemen took this opportunity to replenish their warm brandies. She smiled as she carefully placed the linguini on small plates and added the lobster in sauce on top. The delicious aroma would tempt even the fussiest of eaters and not one person hesitated to dig into their serving.

John's Aunt Julie walked into the room. Her specialty was preparing an English Monkey and she was making certain that no one escaped at least having a taste of it. She had risen quite early this morning more or less in a fog of her own. But after she mixed equal parts of milk and breadcrumbs Julie sat down to enjoy a cup of tea. Soon her eyes were opening and as the thoughts of the events of the day crept into her consciousness an anticipating excitement passed through her body and her awareness blended smoothly with her

enthusiasm to prepare An English Monkey.
She carefully melted butter and stirred in
cheese chunks so the mixture would melt
into a deliciously scented substance. Then
she added the milk and crumb mixture,
beaten eggs, salt and a bit of bicarbonate of
soda. Julie continued to thoroughly mix and
stir the appetizer topping until she was
satisfied with the creamy texture. As Julie
sat the mixture on the stove to keep warm,
she was already planning to make the
wafers, which would carry a bit of An
English Monkey to the guests. A most
palatable treat. And now as she placed a
platter of them on the table in the library
with the Lobster Fettuccini, she caught a
whiff of wine and brandy in the air.

"Perhaps we 'd better move it along," she said. "John and Rita will be opening their gifts soon…and the cake will be served."

"You are right, Julie. People are so comfortable I doubt they will want to leave," answered Emma.

As the two ladies closed the door on their way out they each once again commented to the gentlemen about the time.

"Oh," said Emma as Julie latched the door behind them. "It is so wonderful the way they describe New York. A brand new life just filled with excitement."

"Yes," agreed Julie, "I do hope we will be able to visit."

Within minutes John and Rita were cutting the wedding cake and offering a slice to everyone. They insisted on serving the cake portions themselves. That way they felt a little closer to each and every guest. And each person appreciated their kindness and all were full of thoughts of these two lovely people moving to America to fulfill their dreams.

"We must open the gifts, Husband," whispered Rita when the cake was almost completely gone.

John, startled a bit by his new title, quickly settled and gently stroking Rita's face muttered, "Yes, of course, Mrs. Rodgers."

Together they were trembling with a combination of excitement and exhaustion but they weren't about to let it show to any of their guests. They even seemed to think in unison.

What on earth could possibly be in all these packages? Surely everybody knows we can't take much with us to America. One trunk had been assigned to hold linens, towels, glassware, dishes and silver. It had been quite an ambitious undertaking getting all those treasures into that one trunk, too. It took a lot of wrapping and coaxing followed by more wrapping and even some pleading as though each piece would suddenly cooperate and slide gently into a hidden space meant just for it. But once the trunk was closed, it was locked securely and nothing in God's creation would persuade anyone to open it again.

John and Rita remained puzzled by these beautiful packages so delicately wrapped. It was obvious that the contents of each one had been handled lovingly and treated with great care. Then as they began opening them the concept of the gifts slowly started to materialize in front of them.

They shared the duties of removing tiny ribbons from each package and ever so gently unwrapping the surprise. Each one contained a carefully home made Christmas ornament. They were all made with materials of appropriate colors and each represented a glorious winter scene for the holidays. And they were all stuffed with cotton making them feel soft and pliable.

"How perfect!" Rita could barely speak. "We will always have room for these."

"They are so very special," commented John. "Look at this one. It is shaped like a boy on a sled with 1897 sewn into the runner. It so reminds me of my own childhood. I shall never part with these."

The warmth and emotion spread through the room and many became teary as they pictured the newlyweds enjoying their first holiday together in a far away land. It all represented perfection.

CHAPTER 4

On December 29, 1897, after spending a few days alone in a London Hotel, Mr. and Mrs. John Rodgers boarded the *AUGUSTE VICTORIA* to set sail for America. The schedule was to arrive in New York in twenty days.

"We are finally off, Husband," sighed Rita as they joined the other passengers waving to friends and relatives who had come to bid farewell.

The fog had lifted somewhat as though the weather too was blessing their union and the couples expedition into a new land.

"What an interesting history our ship has," commented John after they had settled into their first class cabin. He was reading the literature left on the desk while Rita was feeling a little green around the gills.

"The *AUGUSTA VICTORIA* was built by Vulcan of Stettin in 1889 and was actually the first express liner to be built in a German shipyard. She was 7650 tons with a size of 461 feet by 56 feet. She was supposed to have the name *NORMANIA*, but with Emperor William II assuming the throne she was named after his consort. The name was actually misspelled until she went in for major alterations."

"We seem to be having a smooth sail now," offered Rita. "I guess I just felt a bit ill at the initial shock of being afloat."

"Yes, it should be smoother now," John continued to read. "Her weight was increased to 8500 tons and her name was corrected."

"Correcting a name makes for smoother sailing?" Rita teased John but secretly she was proud of him for collecting information they could later share with their students. It gave her spirits a lift and she felt much better when she noticed him tucking the papers into one of their suitcases.

Rita picked up a small soft leather satchel and gently held it in her lap as she sat on the bed. John noticed her actions and moved to sit next to his wife.

"What have you in such a beautiful but small satchel? It is so very light. Much like a feather. Is it our most prized possessions?"

Now John was doing the teasing. He knew very well the satchel contained the most precious of all their gifts.

"Would you like to look at them again?" asked Rita as she ever so gently slipped the clasp off its hinge.

Together they, again, carefully reviewed the precious Christmas ornaments. Indeed the entire satchel was as light as a feather and small enough to sit discreetly on a lap. Rita emptied the contents onto the bed and except for a few murmurs about how each carefully crafted item reminded them of their own childhood experiences the room became noiseless and their surroundings unnoticeable. As they fondly wrapped and replaced the last ornament into the satchel the ship suddenly lurched as though they were traversing a very bumpy road.

Rita quickly grasped the satchel and exclaimed, "Oh, I don't want them damaged by the ocean waters! We must keep them safe!"

John laughed, "This ship will never sink, Dear One. We are all safe."

Rita felt gratified with John's presence. His calm soothing voice always had a serene effect on her. "I would like a breath of fresh air. Let's investigate this ship you are so proud of and see what we can discover first hand."

"Fresh air will be of benefit to both of us I should say, Mrs. Rodgers."

So, very much bundled against the December weather the two of them set out to explore the *AUGUSTE VICTORIA*. It would after all be their home for the next three weeks.

"I feel like a child awed by a new experience," said John.

"It is a bit like our respective childhoods. Remember what fun it was to discover what was behind every nook and cranny?"

"The seeking and pouncing was the best game we ever had."

As they stepped onto the deck they became even more aware of the throbbing and vibrating motion caused by the engines and propellers.

"Wonder if we shall adjust to these rhythmic sounds as we travel through the sea," queried John.

"I should think so," answered Rita, "but after 20 days we shall have to adjust to not having those sounds and movements. I'm certain something will be missing when we try to sleep."

"First things first, Mrs. Rodgers. Let's get through the next three weeks before we worry about what isn't around us."

"John, you seem so worried. What is this ominous forthcoming event I hear in your tone of voice?"

"Oh, no I didn't mean anything by it. Not at all. I'm merely adjusting to our new surroundings," John sighed. Yet he knew and felt the presence of an eeriness that seemed to capture him. He really had no idea why he had made that statement or where it really originated. It seemed to have materialized and verbalize itself without warning.

Rita had a watchful eye on her husband and noticed an ever so slight twinge in his facial features. *I wonder…it must be the identical feeling of dread I experienced at the wedding. What on earth could it be? And does he know more?* She shivered a bit and then continued their walk.

The grimness was stifled again, but this time it remained just under the surface of happier thoughts. It was as though it was casting long scary shadows from the sunniest of places.

"Well, I already mentioned this ship was built in 1889. Almost ten years old," John said trying to contain the quiver in his voice.

"Yes, you did," answered Rita who seemed to be regrouping quicker.

They strode quietly for a few moments in the brisk air. Just as John was about to point out what must be the dining area a sudden lurch sideways of the ship brought them both to realize their location. All thoughts escaped them as they struggled for balance. A steward, seemingly nonplused by the situation, calmly made his way past them.

"Steward!" John's voice was demanding.

"Yes, sir?"

"What is this tossing about?"

The steward looked bored as though he had patiently explained this situation a million or more times previously. Other passengers, while also struggling to maintain their footing, joined Rita and John and watched as the steward let his legs absorb the shocks and movements of the ship.

The steward casually explained, "We are in for a few days of weather, I fear.

Perhaps all of you would be a bit more comfortable in your cabins. We will be happy to deliver tea promptly followed by meals and whatever else you may want to drink. It will also provide you an opportunity to plan to investigate the ship on a day more conducive to walking about."

He's reading our minds. Are we that predictable? wondered Rita.

Everyone heeded the steward's advice and slowly made their way back to their cabins.

"Let's review and plan our actions. When the storm passes we will be the most efficient couple on board," suggested John.

"I hadn't realized how the time spent. The hot tea will be most welcome. As we sip our tea we could review the literature."

"We are so fortunate," offered John after they had settled to enjoy their hot tea. "It talks here of the advantages of a steamer. They carry refrigeration and offer all sorts of delicacies for better feeding arrangements. However, they also say there is a feeling of dust and soot on everything you touch on deck."

"We'll worry about that when we are on deck!" blurted Rita. "For now let's order dinner and cozy up for the night. The storm will add to the motions, but we will be safe in each other's arms. If the Auguste Victoria should capsize we will be together."

"It won't capsize...we are safe. But, I must say, if a storm can precipitate a cozier atmosphere accompanied by snuggling then I am all for it."

Their giggles left them both more relaxed as though all their cares had vanished.

Darkness enveloped the steamer as the storm added a slight but tolerable rolling motion.

The steward was right. There would be plenty of time to allot to investigating the ship later.

CHAPTER 5

"I'll take that! I'll carry it myself!"
It was a demand from Rita. She grabbed
the soft leather satchel from seemingly mid-
air as it was being transferred from one
porter to another. Then she realized the
hostility in her attitude and softened her
voice in an effort to explain, "It's as light as
a feather and it fits comfortably in my lap."

John, startled by his wife's outburst,
spoke as calmly as he could, "We are here,
Mrs. Rodgers. This is New York. We are to
begin our dream here."

"I'm so very sorry, dear. It has been such a long three weeks aboard a ship and add a bit of unexpected seasickness...well, I guess I am a little tense. I am certain I will feel better and become a nicer person after I get some rest. I truly apologize for my outburst."

"Everybody understands, Ma'am," offered one of the porters. "We are grateful ourselves to be here."

"See dear, you are not the only one who thinks it was a dreary crossing. The weather, though it did calm, became unbearable in the fog. I fear we saw little of the ship after all. And the fog only seemed to dampen the soot and the grime. It is no wonder we are all a bit cross."

Although Rita was near tears, she became calmed once again by her husband's kind and soothing words. At times during the crossing she felt as though she were on a ghost ship. Figures of other passengers drifted in and out of their sight as though they were mere figures of people. There was nowhere to escape the damp surroundings that they had so hoped to leave at home in London. It wasn't long before day and night blended into one continuous melodramatic experience. John had to constantly remind Rita that at least the ship was moving forward. The inclimate conditions had not worsened so much as to halt the voyage. And, of course, now that they were disembarking the weather was clear even though colder than expected.

"It rained all New Year's Eve but it was still a huge celebration," explained Ben trying to liven the spirits of a very tired couple.

Ben had been chosen by the townspeople to meet Mr. and Mrs. John Rodgers and personally escort them to their new home. It was an honor indeed to be trusted with such an obligation. He had barely reached the age of twenty, but reflected the maturity of one who had already entered the world of haberdashery with the town's most respected business person. The fact that he was anxious to please the new arrivals was so overwhelmingly evident that Rita and John looked with amazement at this charming fellow. Besides, his own wife was due to deliver their first child in a few months and Ben himself had been in the sometimes heated exchanges in discussions on a new schoolhouse and who would administer the teaching duties.

He had left Hunters Point yesterday with the finest pair of horses and the very best carriage in town. Yesterday because he wanted to rest the horses overnight in the local stable. Besides, he wanted to again polish the metal rings and buckles as well as make the leather soft. *Those Londoners will know we do not go without comforts.*

This morning he had groomed the horses as they ate their breakfast and even the equines seemed to be aware of something special in the air. They pricked their ears as each hoof was lifted for a thorough inspection to ensure secure footing on the snowy way home. Then their muscles quivered as they were harnessed. They were ready to put forth their best effort.

"It will be an all day trip," said Ben. "Perhaps we should go now. Lucky the *AUGUSTE VICTORIA* docked when it did; we should reach your new home about dark."

John slid into the front seat while Rita perched on some luggage behind the two men. There was plenty of room for her on the back seat, but she wanted to sit close so she could hear all the news about their new home. John was anxious to hear also and Ben was equally excited to tell them all about it.

"I'm sorry you had such an unpleasant voyage across the ocean," Ben began. "But let me assure you your new home will be most comfortable. It is on some prime tillable land; five acres but about half of that is forest. You will be situated near the water and the new schoolhouse is right across the road. We built the new schoolhouse in a location so most of the children will not have such a trek of it to school and their return home. We voted on the entire process and decided that your home and the new school would be well worth it for the education it will provide."

"Where is it located in relationship to town?" queried John.

"Oh. Quite close. Walking distance. And we have a railroad station, too, but I wanted to drive you so we could talk. Do you have any particular thoughts about how you want to teach?"

"Oh. Yes, indeed!" Answered Rita. "We want to teach and hopefully spark an imagination of inventiveness. The world is changing so rapidly we feel we must all adjust and move forward with it."

Ben giggled; then guffawed out loud, "You are so right," he finally was able to say. "The entire Hunters Point population will be happy to know we did not make an error in judgment when we hired you. I do wish though that you had been here for New Year's Eve. That event is what really brought us all together."

"Oh, we had heard something about it. It must have been a special gala. Were you yourself present for the celebration?" asked John.

"Yes, we were. A group of us traveled to view the parade. We enjoyed it immensely even though it poured rain throughout the night. Oh, what an exciting occasion...actually seeing New York become the second largest city in the whole world right before our eyes. London, of course, remains the absolute largest city in the world. By the way, how is your home town?"

Rita and John responded in unison and without pause, "DEPRESSING!"

"Unbelievable fog, deprecating living conditions for too many Londoners and all with an underlying sense of doom," explained John.

"Yes. One must struggle to achieve and maintain an optimistic attitude," offered Rita absently. She was thinking back to the strange eerie feelings that had prompted the shivers in her. Then as she turned and gazed at Ben in wonderment she became convinced the ominous feelings had been nothing more than a passing dot of gloom. A most temporary of extraneous feelings to invade a person's life without warning and easily explained away with current circumstances.

Ben is so upbeat and positive, she thought. *Surely the future is as we have hoped.*

She relaxed a bit with a sigh as she turned back towards her husband and commented almost in a whisper, "We are so grateful."

"It might be cold, but the future remains bright and sunny," John was agreeing with his wife.

Then John regrouped from his far away hazy look and addressed their newfound friend, "Tell us more about New Year's Eve. Were there many people present to witness the birth of such extraordinary history?"

"Oh, yes. It was estimated the crowd numbered about 100,000. Every one of its members was huddled under umbrellas. Soon, before midnight, we broke into a chorus of *Auld Lang Syne*. Then everything became quite hushed and silent as we waited in anticipation of the most remarkable event.

The mayor in San Francisco pushed a button, which sent electricity our way lighting our array of brightly colored lights and raising our Greater New York flag. We all roared with excitement with such a din that we barely heard the one hundred cannon salute. Countless skyrockets were sent aloft and we suddenly became one great big city. Just think of the massive consolidation of Brooklyn, Queens, Staten Island, Manhattan, and the Bronx into Greater New York. It all happened on January first, eighteen hundred and ninety eight and we were there as witnesses." Ben was obviously proud to be a Greater New

Yorker. The thrill of it all lingered with him and gave him an aura rarely observed by anyone.

Rita listened with an interest so intense she did not realize she was caressing, stroking and alternately squeezing the small satchel in her lap.

Her eyes became misty as she gazed into the distance in an attempt to picture the celebration and how it would all fit into their lives. If ever she had any doubts about their ambitious move here they were banished. There was no way any ominous thought could interfere with her perception of their future. Yes, Mr. and Mrs. John Rodgers were free to enjoy the life they chose to live in the second largest city in the world. But what was even more impressive was the warm welcome from the people of Hunters Point, New York. In the Queens. Her happiness would sustain her throughout the final miles to their new home. Even the brisk cold air seemed to help define the warmth they felt.

John with his ever-analytical mind drawing on facts to digest and later share, pointed out interesting features on a map as they traced their route.

"Look, dear, we have options on modes of transport to and from Hunters Point. Carriage, railroad or by water. Travel is so convenient here."

They both felt their horizons broadening and squeezed hands with a thrill passing between them. Also between them

were the Christmas ornaments so dear to
both their hearts.

CHAPTER 6

Ben had been a bit off in his timing or maybe they were slower than they should have been since the scenery and the pleasantness of the ride lulled them into a state of bliss. No matter how it happened, it was dark when they arrived at their destination of Hunters Point.

"Your new home is no doubt cold and will need a fire started. Why not spend tonight in our one hotel with dinner on us. I know the townsfolk won't mind; they will be so happy you are here. It is warm and you will be able to rest while we take your luggage to your home."

It wasn't difficult to convince John and Rita that they needed to rest. The long trip was obviously wearing on them. Without a hint of dissatisfaction they alit from the carriage and stepped into the Hunters Point Hotel.

"Ben is such a pleasant person," said Rita as they settled into their hotel room with bare necessities. Then she added, "I am so proud we made the move to New York."

"I totally agree with you, dear. But right now what we need most is some rest. It creates an especially friendly feeling knowing our personal belongings await us in our new home for the morrow."

They both realized they must stop and rest if they planned to be of any use in the days ahead.

John took a deep breath and exhaled audibly.

"What is it dear husband? Something wrong?"

"No. Everything is right now. I am going to drift off to a restful sleep with a small serene farm pictured in my mind...like I always dreamt about as a child. Of course farming itself is foreign to me but since only good pictures are permitted in sleepy thoughts I know all will go well."

Rita snuggled a little closer and confessed her thoughts, too. "I will be projecting a picture of our new home with a school house across the road. Lots of children romping about with inquiring minds."

A peaceful sleep did envelope them like a gentle drift into a new serene atmosphere.

The breakfast they were served the following morning was an extension of the welcome they had felt on arrival.

"Yes, sir." Dan the proprietor was speaking, "It sure is a blessing to welcome a couple of teachers to this area. We had advertised for weeks and about gave up on finding even one teacher. Two is definitely a blessing. Hunters Point is swelling to seven thousand people and our offspring are bright and eager to learn. With all the newness—even a new century soon—we need to keep up so we can grasp the opportunity to spring ahead. Our children are our best resources for an innovative leap into a new era. Oh, I'm sorry. Your accommodations satisfactory?"

"Yes. Quite," replied John.

"I'm hoping to expand as the population demands," Dan went on as the new couple munched on their breakfast. "I know its small now with the store attached, but the dry goods is what keeps me afloat."

"Your dry goods are important to the community and yours offer a good selection for a town this size. Perhaps there is a woolen mill nearby. That would make your selections more complete and comfortable for those who live here," Rita was a bit demanding which was her way of pushing towards the future.

Dan appeared miffed and backed away.

John took Rita's hand and led her outdoors. "Shall we walk? Or would you prefer to ride? We can get a carriage, I'm certain. I would like to walk myself. The boards on the walkways look stable and the light dusting of snow has been removed by a gentle breeze."

"Alright, Husband. Let's walk. It will be good for both of us since we have been pent up for so long. Exercise will be of benefit, certainly."

"Rita, please do not be offended but I feel I must say to you...well, just to mention slightly dear...about your comments. We do want to avoid assuming the roles of bossy know-it-alls. We want to make a good impression that simply means we want to blend in with our surroundings. After all, these are people who trust us with their children's learning experiences. We cannot nor do we want to run the whole town by criticizing what they have or don't possess."

They walked quietly for a bit. Rita held tightly to her husband's arm. She thought if she let go the whole world would know she was shaken. First she had spoken sharply to Ben while he was being so kind; now the proprietor of one of the main businesses in Hunters Point was the object of her criticism. A woolen factory will arrive in due time. She hadn't needed to mention it. But she came from the largest city in the world and it was perfectly natural for her to miss the conveniences the stores offered in London. John was right, of course. She would have to be more cautious about what she said no matter how much she wanted Hunters Point to mirror London.

She squeezed his arm as tightly as she could as she blinked her eyes rapidly. There was some discomfort in her throat—a feeling she had rarely experienced in her lifetime—that told her not everyone was to become her disciple. Just because she had had a nice comfortable background didn't mean she could force her ideas on everyone. Now Rita realized she had more than a lot to learn.

They continued to walk in silence. Both were digesting the ambience of this town and they passed stores that offered anything they would possibly need.

John with all his suave, debonair style paused long enough to touch his wife's face. Then he whispered, "Don't forget, Love. New York City isn't so far away should we want to visit a large metropolis to remind us of home."

It was at that precise moment they both realized they had stepped onto a snow covered cross street. There was nothing more than a slight give in the snow under their weight, but it was enough to remind them they were no longer afloat.

Ground! Earth! Soil changed their mood immediately to one of fantastic joy.

Neither could contain their laughter as they imagined what picture they were portraying to the local inhabitants as they quickened their step to the next walkway.

Shortly John turned to his wife and said, "Here, Mrs. Rodgers, is our new home. Not a far walk at all."

"Yes, it was a mere trek. Oh, it looks like a warm inviting cottage. It looks like home...our home."

They were both a bit giddy as they entered the front door. Even though it was a small but cozy cottage it represented room and space to them. Freedom for their thoughts to flourish. It was all they would need to secure the happiness they had planned.

John started a fire in the stove as Rita busied herself with unpacking. As she unwrapped each piece of glassware she realized each one of them represented heartbreak if it were broken. Rita took a deep breath and let out a long sigh. Then she cast away any doubts by remembering all the help she'd had packing and she knew her treasures would be safe even through a rough sea voyage and a somewhat bumpy ride to their new home.

"It's a nice place," commented John as he noticed the faraway look in his wife's eye. "Here, let me help you with that. It will be toasty in here in short time."

"I feel the warmth in here already. This glassware has arrived in tact. The workmanship on these cabinets is beautiful." Rita was running on without hesitation.

When everything was proper, they walked outside to view the small empty barn and a chicken coop.

"We can borrow enough tools to start our farming project."

"Let's investigate the schoolhouse Irregardless of the snow and the mud I think I shall love it here."

"We both will," John's whispery voice asserted.

The schoolhouse consisted of rows of seats with writing desks and a large desk for the teacher.

Almost defiantly Rita vowed, "It's a start. We will improve it."

CHAPTER 7

Rita sat on the edge of the bed crying so intensely she was intermittently experiencing heaves. They had been settled for only one week and everything had been going so well for them. She turned towards her husband and all she could muster was a guttural scream directed at him for causing such turmoil. She continued holding her stomach as though the profoundness of the pain could be soothed with mere noise.

Then she kept repeating, "Why? Why? Why?"

It took hours for John to console her.

"Dear," he said, "you have been a bundle of nerves for quite a while. Ever since our wedding day. Now those dark ominous feelings are out where we can both deal with them."

"John, you are not being realistic. You simply can't walk off and leave me."

"I am not leaving you, my dear one. I am going on a temporary voyage to help bring peace to this part of the world. Don't you realize how important it will be to me— to us—that people know I want to support our new country?"

"But the possibility of war…"

"…is remote." John finished the sentence for her.

"The newspapers," John went on, "are full of talk about war, but President McKinley is striving for peace."

"Oh, John. Don't you understand? Everyone is tense with anticipation and many feel war is better than the suspense."

"All the more reason to be devoted to peace, my dear. You are doing so well with the school. Remember how you wanted to improve it yourself? It will be a major project for you and I shan't be in the way to argue with such a determined yet beautiful wife. And besides, I will no doubt be returning for Spring—in time, I should say, to prepare our farm for planting. Oh, we will certainly be on top of the world."

"We don't need the whole world, Husband. But you paint such a glorious

85

picture it is difficult to argue. I can see it as an opportunity to catapult ourselves into a most rewarding position."

Rita was sobbing and near exhaustion. Maybe she was too tired to think and besides deep inside she wanted so much to please her husband.

"The Spanish know they cannot win a war with us. They are trying so hard to avoid any conflict at all. And to help with the peace, now we have the American Consul in Cuba recommending a friendly American ship be harbored in Havana."

"Very well, John. You have had such reliable sense and logic ever since I've known you, I can see no reason to doubt you now. But you do promise to be back in the spring don't you? After all you are the farmer in the family."

"Yes, indeed. I am so looking forward to my return. More than you know."

"Apparently there is no reason for alarm. By the way what is the name of the vessel you will be aboard?"

"The Maine. Sets sail the day after tomorrow. Ben and Dan are both going as well. We need to be at the railroad station on the morrow and prepared to travel to New York Harbor."

Each of their wives had settled into a state that enabled them to disguise their few sobs with careful coughs. Ben's wife actually had the hic-coughs when they arrived at the railroad station.

Rita was especially calm and serene. She had come to understand her husband was pursuing a determination that had originated deep inside of him.

It was, after all, an honorable quest for recognition and ultimately the school itself could benefit. Besides, it would give her a chance to organize the school and improve the selections of reading materials. But most important of all she would plan the warmest of welcome home for her husband.

Even the climate would have to cooperate. Rita had already planned to work through Ben's wife to secure all the tools they would need to start farming. She would seek advice about crops and chicken feed. It would all be prepared to the last detail. But the most precious gift of all for John would be his wife waiting for him when he returned.

Our plans have worked out so far. Why not this one? Oh, it will be a most wonderful reunion. Rita thought as she waved goodbye to John.

John sat quietly on the train with Ben and Dan. They were all reflecting on their return in the spring.

On January 25, 1898 the twenty-four-gun battleship *Maine* anchored in Havana harbor. John Rodgers was one of the men aboard. He had become fast friends with Dan and Ben, the three of them finding excitement in the air as they talked about their part in avoiding a war with Spain.

On the night of February 15, the three friends were passing time playing poker. At about 9:30 PM John arose from his seat and excused himself saying, "My legs are in dire need of stretching as is the rest of my body. Besides the both of you are enjoying winning streaks. Would you care to join me for a walk around the bulkhead?"

Ben thought for a moment and then declined the offer saying he was unaccustomed to the sultry heat of Havana. Dan agreed with Ben saying it was simply too hot to be out and about. Their perspiration was heavy enough to have soaked their shirts, which they had removed much earlier.

John casually donned his yet damp shirt and stretched his muscles. Then he walked towards the bulkhead thinking of all the excitement of sharing information about a real battleship with his soon to be students. He reminded himself that President McKinley continued to work towards peace with Spain and, to insure that possibility, they should all be willing to remain where they were for as long as it takes. However, there was an ache inside of him for Rita. Oh, how he missed her.

At 9:40 PM, just minutes after John left the card game, the Maine exploded and of the 350 officers and men aboard 260 were killed. John and Rita had had a perfect wedding with a bright future less than two months prior to his disintegration from the flames of the explosion.

91

Dan received minor burns, but would recover. Ben was uninjured and the two of them were sent home to Hunters Point. There they would go with their wives to see Rita.

"Remember the Maine. Remember the Maine. That is all I hear or see in print anymore." Rita was to numb to think and the grief was so extreme she had not shed a tear. John's body was vaporized. She would have no physical touch with the tragedy. There was a brief memorial service but it left her with an empty feeling as though her husband would soon return.

If only they would stop advertising the tragedy with that incessant message: Remember the Maine.

She had already gathered some of the tools for farming and she became obsessed with keeping them handy.

"John will need them when he..." It seemed all her sentences started like that and ended with her thinking *Remember the Maine.*

So worried were her friends that they persuaded Rita to move back to Dan's hotel. She agreed only after she remembered to grasp the soft leather satchel containing the cuddly Christmas ornaments they had held so dear. Then she mostly sat in her room with the satchel nestled safely in her lap.

It was Ben's wife who finally came up with a solution to the problems at hand.

"Remember our celebration on New Years Eve?" She was addressing the others out of earshot of Rita. "It was the mayor of San Francisco who sent the electric pulse that raised our new flag. Maybe he could help a widow whose husband gave his life in an effort to obtain peace."

"You may have an excellent idea," Dan mused aloud. "She wants to continue their dream of teaching, but it would become unbearable here. With the newspapers screaming 'Remember the *Maine*' and no doubt war declared soon...well, it would just be too much for her."

They promptly sent a wire and received a reply from the mayor himself. He would have a special welcome for Rita and even help her find suitable living arrangements. "San Francisco needs teachers and we are especially interested in the ones with futuristic plans," were the last words on his message.

Her friends packed her belongings as carefully as John and Rita had unpacked them. Then they used the finest carriage to escort her to the same railroad station where she had last seen John. But this time Rita insisted she should personally hold the soft leather satchel.

CHAPTER 8

Everything was happening too fast for Rita. Here she was traveling in a Pullman car of luxury while it seemed like yesterday she was planning a homecoming for her gallant husband, John.

"Mrs. Rodgers?" It was the conductor talking. "We want you to be comfortable for this entire trip. Please try to rest and let us know if you need anything."

Rita was trying to collect her thoughts. Not everything she heard was sinking into her brain. It took her a few moments to realize her location. The rhythmic sounds and sway of the train was reminiscent of the ocean voyage a few weeks ago. Her thought process was nebulous as she struggled to retain some sense of sanity.

Perhaps, she thought, *if I make every effort to meet people and remember all I can about them it will be therapy for me. I keep expecting John to walk through the door.*

"Your name please," she said to the conductor.

"Andrew, ma'am. Is there anything I can do for you?"

"Yes. I was wondering about meals. Where is the dining car?"

"Oh. Simply walk through that door. It is located in the next car. Of course, we can have your meals delivered to you here if you wish. I'm sure you'll be happy with our selections."

"Thank you. I think I'll decide at each mealtime. This car—it's so luxurious. Are my items on board also?"

Rita worried that she was making no sense at all but even the slightest bit of control would give her something of a basis to re-erect her strong will.

"Yes, ma'am," Andrew was trying to guide her into a positive thought process. "Your possessions are aboard. We can bring them in here if you prefer."

"No. That won't be necessary. As long as I'm reassured of their safe location."

"Yes, ma'am."

"Will we be making any transfers anywhere? I haven't had time to study my ticket."

"Yes, ma'am. But you needn't worry. You are set until we reach San Francisco. Others will be transferring at various places. Especially Chicago. We usually take on a lot of passengers there."

"Oh. And will you be going on?"

"Yes, ma'am. I will be available to aid you for the entire trip."

"I'm rather overwhelmed with this car. I never expected anything so roomy."

"I hear that comment a lot. It is certainly made for comfort. The two easy chairs on each side swivel so you can enjoy the full view."

"I noticed the windows are so expansive. That will help."

"Help? Ma'am? Are you alright?"

There was a long pause. Rita was trembling and near tears. She regained her composure but it took a few minutes as Andrew helped her sit down and offered her a glass of water. He was genuinely concerned and asked again, "Are you alright? You said something about help. I'm sorry I didn't quite understand your words."

Rita realized she had been babbling. *Will this foggy feeling ever lighten?*

After a few moments Rita turned to Andrew and explained her feelings. "It's just that the movement of the train and the sounds remind me of the voyage we experienced on our honeymoon. Our trip to America with all our dreams. Now I realize what a big help it is to gaze out the expansive windows to see the settlements and people going about their business."

"I know the feeling of needing people, but I myself have also found a hobby to be most rewarding. It seems I spend too much time on these trips away from my family and I know tolerating the passage of time can be difficult."

Rita was suddenly interested.

"Hobby? Please tell me about your hobby."

"Only after you agree to a meal. You must be famished with all the activities you have experienced lately."

"Very well. An early dinner would suit me fine. Can you join me? I'd much prefer having a meal here in my quarters since I am not at all trusting of my lightheadedness."

"Yes, ma'am." Andrew was proud of his ability to reach out to persons in distress. The railroad bosses knew it too and they gave him freedom ordinarily denied to employees. So many people had commended the line for having him available to aid them that Andrew had literally described his own job.

"You will have a chance to freshen while I prepare a couple of dinner trays," commented Andrew as he slipped out the door.

Rita was grateful for the few minutes alone. She took a deep breath and let it out slowly pursing her lips. Then she straightened her hair and mused clothes. She also splashed some water onto her face.

A few minutes later she was sitting opposite Andrew with a luscious dinner in front of her. The aroma of the food touched and awakened some hunger pangs.

No wonder I am so shaky. I simply do not recall my last meal. Have I been dazed for that long?

Andrew began to slowly eat his dinner as he carefully watched Rita devour hers. Only when he was convinced she would take the nourishment did he begin to speak.

"Yes, ma'am. I have a beautiful wife and three children at home in San

Francisco. Can't wait to see them—never can. So each stop the train makes gives me an opportunity to locate some wood pieces to carve. Sometimes I can even find pieces of bone for scrimshaw. I carve pictures on it to depict a scene and stain it with ink. Usually I like to do scenes that help identify the location where it was found. If, for some reason I can't, then I simply write the location somewhere on it."

Between the good foods that seemed to sooth her frazzled being and the melodious voice of Andrew telling his story, Rita became more alert and her thinking began to clear.

"What an outstanding idea," she said with an obvious lift in her voice. "Your family must treasure your gifts."

"Yes, ma'am. They display them at all times. Some of the items have their names and birth dates engraved on them. They seem to appreciate that thought even more than the final picture."

"I understand the attraction. It must be quite a celebration each time you return home from a trip."

"Yes, ma'am. I do wish I could obtain gainful employment near home. I do miss them so. Each time I am away they look for ads and keep any interesting ones for me to scour through."

Rita began to realize how important it was for her to take charge of her own destiny. She would never forget John and his memory would be included in all her tasks. She would definitely pursue teaching with the vigor of two people.

"I wish the best for you—and your family as well," she said to Andrew.

"Yes, ma'am. Thank you ma'am." Andrew was busy collecting dishes and stacking them on a tray. It was obvious to him Mrs. Rodgers was feeling better but a bit drowsy. As he quietly left her alone he hoped she would rest tonight. A good night of rest always made things look better in the morning.

Rita, alone now, carefully prepared her bed. It was a bit early yet but the tiredness was tugging at her. It turned out Andrew was right again. As soon as she laid her head on the pillow she was serenely enveloped by a peaceful uninterrupted sleep.

In the morning Rita dressed and faced the world with an optimism she had not felt since she had last seen John. She was, after all, on an adventure and would arrive in San Francisco in a few days.

She felt light with a gradual building of energy in her body. But most of all she felt anxious to see her new home and start teaching.

CHAPTER 9

Spring was definitely in the California air when Rita stepped from the comfort of her Pullman car to the busy railroad station. A slight breeze swarmed around her as if asking permission to lighten her spirits.

Rita closed her eyes to enjoy the atmosphere and allowed her mind to drift into a most pleasant state. When she opened them she saw a placard held by a young couple. The placard read 'Mrs. Rita Rodgers'. She stood amidst the bustle and raised her arm. It only took a moment for her to catch their eye and for them to respond with a recognizable nod. Then they slowly made their way to Rita. Rita noticed there weren't two but three people to greet her: a gentleman and two ladies.

"We are so happy to meet you. I am Carol Stuart. This is my husband Joseph and my sister, Eileen. Joseph will gather your belongings and place them in the carriage. May I help you carry something?" Carol was motioning towards Rita's arms.

"No!" avowed Rita. Then she caught herself when she noticed her three greeters were taken aback. *What am I doing in San Francisco and who are these people?* she wondered.

"I'm sorry," Rita spoke softly. "I've done considerable traveling of late and feel a bit edgy. My satchel may appear awkward but it is actually so very light and soft I find it no bother at all to carry."

"We understand, Mrs. Rodgers. Perhaps what you need at this point is some time to settle and acclimate to your new environment. I'll take your heavy luggage now to the carriage."

"We will be sharing the same boarding house," offered Eileen. "I am a teacher also and look forward to sharing ideas with you."

"My husband works for the city. He helps describe boundaries. San Francisco is growing so rapidly. Anyway we were so delighted when he received the assignment to meet you at the station and aid in your settling," explained Carol.

They all sat comfortably in the carriage while the two horses moved at a leisurely pace.

"Did you know, Mrs. Rodgers, that America plans to acquire Hawaii this year? We don't know how that will influence our population, but we try to be prepared for any eventuality," spoke Joseph. He was trying to describe his work duties. Then he went on. "We here in San Francisco pride ourselves in our diversity. Not long ago there was terrible discrimination towards others, but now we have become accustomed to equality. I'm trying to present you with a bit of background so you shan't be astonished later. Equality is our goal."

It was difficult to believe they had been plodding along for hours. They had become so warm to each other and Rita was experiencing a superior feeling of absolutely no reservations about her move to San Francisco.

They had talked about the first public school in San Francisco and it's opening in 1849. The support for schools, libraries and museums came from the silver mine fortunes made in Nevada. A great deal of support also came from the riches made by the California railroad kings. There would be plenty of money to improve the schools and learning materials would be available upon request. The entire city, it seemed, wanted their offspring prepared for the future. California was indeed a golden state that offered opportunities for everyone.

There was a place called Nob Hill where the wealthy built mansions. They had their own way of doing education for their children, but they continued to support public schools for everyone. It was the grandest of ideas and Rita became increasingly excited about the prospects of teaching.

Although it seemed like a short time had lapsed, their carriage rolled up to the front of a house in the North Beach part of San Francisco.

"This is your new home, Mrs. Rodgers. The owners are anxious to meet you and they promise comfort."

"And I know you will be comfortable. I have found it offers all anyone could need," said Eileen.

"I'm sorry. I've forgotten to ask all of you to call me Rita. I've been so immersed in your details about this area."

"Well done then, Rita. I'll transfer your baggage to your room while you get acquainted with your new landlord."

Mr. and Mrs. Robert Sands were indeed delighted to meet Rita and Mrs. Sands brewed a special tea for them to enjoy as the men cared for the luggage. It wasn't long before all of them were settled in the parlor with various snacks to accompany their tea.

"Robert works in construction," said Mrs. Sands. "And, oh, please call me Zelda. I really do not care for formalities."

"My schedule," explained Robert, "is so busy that I fear I will not be able to chat as frequently as I would like. With all the influx of people to this area housing has become rather scarce, but we are struggling to produce adequate residential areas for everyone. I do hope you plan to remain in this area. What a definite need we have for teachers."

"Oh, I am so pleasantly surprised by the warm welcome how could I even consider another move. And the idea of living in the heart of a neighborhood with a school so convenient to everyone. I must say I didn't expect it to be so near and with such a large playground. I want so much to investigate the building, but I've lots to do before then. Settling is a big chore in itself."

Joseph and Carol stood and announced, "We must be on our way also but we are confident we are leaving you in the best of care."

Zelda smiled as they left. There was definitely a warmness to this area. Everyone went about their routines, but at the same time remained available to help others.

Eileen offered to help Rita with unpacking and settling in her room upstairs. Rita was happy with the offer and Zelda announced she would begin dinner preparations.

Giggles erupted from Rita and Eileen as they traversed the stairs with anticipation of a good relationship. It did promise to be an ideal arrangement and no one was more surprised than Rita to hear herself sounding human.

Rita had not realized San Francisco was so cosmopolitan and beckoned so strongly to entertainers for a performance in one of its theaters. The gold rush had supported drama as well as musical offerings and they were available to all citizens.

Rita turned to Eileen and said, "I so appreciate everything and especially you for helping me. I do wish, however, we could see the school today. I am oh so anxious to get a view of what is offered. Perhaps you wouldn't mind helping me settle later."

"But of course!" Eileen was delighted with the idea. "We shall have plenty of time to settle you. Let's go right now."

They turned and walked back down the steps. Eileen felt a bit embarrassed she hadn't thought of it sooner herself. It was only natural for Rita to be interested in the school. They both still felt happy with laughter as they waved to Zelda and stepped out the door.

The house next door to the school appeared empty and when Rita asked she learned the owner had recently passed away. There were plans to purchase the property, demolish the house and build a library. Rita's hopes soared as they passed by the future site for a library in its very own building and she closed her eyes secretly wishing she could be in on the planning.

Next to the old house was the school. They paused as Rita took in every detail she could. It was a stucco building and quite modern; a sprawling building that seemed to be surrounded on all sides by playground.

"My," she commented to her new friend, "I can hardly wait to see what is indoors."

CHAPTER 10

"It certainly is fitting for the most cosmopolitan city west of the Mississippi," commented Rita.

"I know the supporters of this educational system want to emphasize English grammar. All people agree that it is difficult to work at any profession if one cannot communicate properly. We also offer literature, geography, history and mathematics."

"Oh," chimed in Rita. "I want so much to introduce more. Like the study of the theater. One never knows where a child will blossom. And I would like to see the library equipped for students and adults alike."

"Whoa! Rita! Don't even think of so much at once. This school is to prepare children for working. If they—or their parents—choose to further their education they will be going downtown to a private high school. That is where they will receive indoctrinations into all aspects of life."

"Not if I have my way," Rita mused. "The sooner the better for arts and education."

"These schools house up to the sixth grade. Sometimes only a handful of students are present, but at least they are working on mandatory education. That is the purpose of district schools; so everyone can be touched by them. When they leave here they are no longer children, but they are ready to head out to find gainful employment. The private schools and colleges are costly indeed. I wouldn't expect too much at once."

"Maybe in time. Maybe with diligence and determination we will be able to expand the thinking of all parents to include further education."

"Perhaps we will someday. I must say you have such innovative ideas and I am honored you are sharing them with me."

"Oh. Don't you see? The more education available for all people will result in better lives. And, of course, the more variances we can offer, the better the chances we will touch a genius, or a famous actor or a president or a…"

"Please, Rita. Let's start with what we have and move to a more determined environment later."

"Oh, I am so sorry. Expressing my ultimate dreams so adamantly. Usually I do not display my aggressive behavior, but I miss John so and it was our dream to touch the young mind for further accomplishments. I feel I must work for the two of us."

"I understand and I, too, hope you will realize your dream. And I hope I can work with you along the way. Here, shall we enter the building where it will all start?"

They had been walking along at a leisurely pace with each of them engrossed in their conversation and all the while anxiously waiting to hear more of the other's plans. Now they paused at the main door.

It was really not much more than a one-room school house with walls to define a few rooms. Rita struggled to hide her disappointment. She had expected a larger building with a separate room for each class.

Now she was looking at a building with walls made out of partitions that were practically transparent. Certainly the slightest of noises would travel as an annoyance. The school building was not even being used to its fullest capacity.

Rita turned to her new friend and stuttered, "But I thought...we will need...I expected more room. Teaching is such serious business. How are we to...?"

They are so liberal with their taxation for the educational process, thought Rita. *Surely it won't be difficult to expand this building to accommodate mandatory education for all the classes. After all, California is known for their free schools for their offspring and their wealth to support them. Surely some internal work would not be too much to ask.*

Her friend, Eileen, abruptly interrupted her thoughts.

"I really think we should head back and get you settled. It has been such a long day for you and a good nights rest will benefit us all."

"Yes, you are right," muttered Rita. Suddenly she became aware of the tiredness she felt in her shoulders. She hoped everything would look better tomorrow.

The following morning Rita awoke feeling refreshed and eager to face the day. It was a feeling she had not experienced for a long while and yet the optimism was so familiar to her. She briefly recalled her wedding ceremony and the reception. The guests had been overwhelmingly negative with dire predictions of disasters soon to befall London and the world. Well, just wait until she could write home about the fantastic wealth generated in California.

As if to secure her soaring mood, she was informed at breakfast of a meeting she was expected to attend. The mayor himself would be present as well as others who had direct input into the educational system. She hoped this would be her golden opportunity to voice her dreams. Excitement pulsed through her body as she mentally prepared her delivery of ideas.

When she arrived at the meeting, which was held at the Town Hall, Rita was pleasantly surprised at the cordial reception and politeness of these people. When she was asked to speak her opinion she did so with the feeling of encouragement and without hesitation.

"Our main goal is to spark a young mind and to aid that youngster into a system of thought processes which will enable him to eventually pursue his own goals. In order to make this accomplishment we must offer an atmosphere of learning. Each child must have access to a room to share with a few classmates of the same age. They must be awarded one teacher per room. This set up will permit them to work on basics appropriate to their level of learning. There mustn't be distractions from other aged children who are simultaneously learning at a different level."

Rita paused but only for a moment. Then she stood and paced as she continued. The room had become silent and Rita seemed to enter a different plane as though she was not aware of the presence of any other person. Her audience sat mesmerized waiting for further words from her.

"I truly believe in the concept of neighborhood schools. Next to the school where I am to teach is a boarded up house. It is vacant and there are plans to demolish it. A new library on that spot would be useful, but I would like to see it large enough to offer reading material to the adults of the community as well. I suspect many of them have never had the time or place to spend with books and a potentially avid reader was lost.

"Education can reach beyond the schools and embrace anyone who chooses to learn. We want people of the community to have the desire that school be mandatory for their children. We want them involved and sharing learning experiences is the best way to command support from everyone."

Rita suddenly startled, jerking her head to look at the audience. *Have I overstepped? Why are they so quiet? I didn't realize I had assumed total control of the floor and I'd better not speak anymore else they will think I want control of the entire meeting.*

She quickly apologized for the length of her talk and returned to her seat in an attempt to regain her demur status meant to support the committee's recommendations. Quietly she listened as others discussed playground equipment, school starting times and the item on the agenda which seemed most important to them: time away from classes to help with chores.

Rita wanted to speak again and explain the importance of field trips to a show and introducing music and art, but she knew she had better wait. Those ideas could be offered at a later time.

As she later prepared for her second night in a boarding house, Rita became fully aware of the importance of having the comfort of such nice people around her. Eileen was in a room just down the hall while the owners; Robert and Zelda Sands had their bedroom downstairs. Since they were always up early and moving about they thoughtfully made a separate bedroom for their own selves to avoid waking their boarders.

Rita, meanwhile, thought she could use this opportunity to write a long, informative letter to her parents. She wanted them to not wait to visit her and felt the schools here would be excellent for her brother. Besides with so much turmoil and changes in London, wouldn't it be better for them to live here? Sunshine and silver would solve her father's business ills—if any lingered. The last she had heard the business was beginning to turn around for her parents and they were considering selling it. What perfect timing.

CHAPTER 11

Rita could not have been happier. Her brother had finished high school and, along with their parents, had arrived in San Francisco. It had been seven years since they had seen each other and there was a lot to talk about. Her letters had not done justice to describe her good fortune. She simply had to show them how great her life in a new country was going.

Her father had made a moderate success of his business and sold it when Gary graduated. They were now staying in a hotel in downtown San Francisco while they made plans and acclimated to their new environment. Gary would attend San Francisco State College. Their parents were intensely interested in the arts, but also looked forward to semi-retirement. They wanted to live near a city close to the theaters and colorful influences worldwide.

All of them had an exhaustive, but joyful few days and Rita was grateful to lay her head on her own pillow to secure a good night sleep. Her thoughts were to prepare for tomorrow's activities as she slipped into a deep, restful slumber.

It happened at five o'clock the following morning. The few people who were awake noticed the nervousness of the animals. Normally calm, docile horses were pulling at their harnesses and neighing their anxieties.

Then a deep horrendous rumble came from inside the earth. The prosperous city of San Francisco, which had become world known for its famous cultural offerings and happy lifestyles, was experiencing a devastating earthquake.

The people who were awake at that hour actually saw streets suddenly resemble waves from the ocean. There was no doubt it was an earthquake but few realized the worsening conditions accompanying the after shocks. Most everyone had been tossed from their beds or, if out, knocked to the ground on their backs.

The worst disaster in San Francisco history was suddenly upon its residents and relentlessly toppled buildings and created wide open cracks in the ground, which if viewed from above would resemble lightning bolts searing their way through the earth.

Rita, startled from the enjoyable sleep she had so desperately needed, was perplexed for a few moments.

My I haven't fallen out of bed for many years! She thought.

"Oh, no!" She shouted as she realized the problem "I must reach my family."

After the initial jolt, Eileen staggered down the hallway. She was bleeding from the forehead and obviously had taken a hit from a falling piece of wood. Rita reached for her and together they made their way towards the staircase.

"We must go downstairs. It will be safer there and we can work our way outdoors," said Eileen with a slight slur to her words.

Robert and Zelda stood dazed at the bottom of the stairs. Both were struggling to keep their balance as they grappled for a hand hold on something...anything. Suddenly Robert looked up at the two teachers. After a shockingly long pause he shouted, "No! Don't try using the stairs!"

Rita and Eileen had already stepped forward and stopped with most of their weight resting on the second step. They both realized their mistake as they watched a huge crack in the stairs travel upward at an alarming speed. They barely had time to watch the cracking of the floor travel past them and down the hall when they felt the pull of gravity. Together they tumbled into a heap and came to rest beside their landlord who was struggling to help his wife towards the front door.

As quickly as it started the rumbling stopped. Robert helped both ladies to their feet and out the door to join Zelda. All stood in a state of shock.

"Earthquake! Stay out of the house! It may collapse any moment," ordered Robert.

About the time they were ready to speak the second wave of destruction hit. All four of them were thrown to the ground as though a huge muscular wrestler had lifted them above his head and then followed with a body slam. They all lay there for minutes with their brains trying to scramble some common sense into their heads and ward off panic.

Downtown the devastation continued to take its toll. Bricks were falling from skyscrapers crushing nearby rooming houses. People were frantic as they rushed through the streets. No one could have been prepared. One lone man was seen crawling from the top of a skyscraper. A small crowd had gathered and continued to shout, "STOP! STOP! STOP!" and then followed their plea with a chant of "STOP! DON'T JUMP!" Finally a few men rushed into the building and upstairs in a gallant effort to reach the unknown stranger. It was only when they rushed into a room they realized the hopelessness of the situation. They saw a lady's hand protruding from a pile of bricks. She was still abed. They scrambled to uncover her only to view her dead body. A young man lay quietly on the floor amid bricks which had obviously rendered him unconscious. An ambulance rushed him to a hospital as the workers continued to search for people lost in the rubble. After shocks continued to shake the area but no one wanted to leave.

Fires erupted throughout the city and at one point four square blocks were ablaze. It was all soon thoroughly consumed with embers glowing like an inviting, twinkling reminder of what had been. The lifeless overflowed the morgue.

Rita had struggled to her feet and aided Eileen whose bloodied forehead needed tending. Then they both sat in the front yard of their boarding house weeping. Rita tore the pleated hem of her own gown using it to carefully dab and cleanse her friends forehead. Zelda had managed to re-enter the house and returned with a cup of water and a sliver of soap. Together they managed to accomplish a suitable bandage; then sat back trying to collect their thoughts.

"Where is Robert?" Rita was finally able to speak.

"He's gone back inside. He is determining the extent of the damage to the house. Oh, how fortunate we are to have him here," Zelda spoke through her tears.

"If anyone can repair the damage he can, but I am sick with worry about my sister. Her baby is due soon," Eileen was obviously alert.

Rita thought back to her own arrival in San Francisco. Carol had looked pale and drawn. She was tired and shortly after that she had lost the baby she was carrying. Eileen had reason for her concern. Carol had not looked at all well during this pregnancy and everyone was delighted she had made it this far. They must find a way to get to them and in some way offer what help they could. Rita was glad Eileen was thinking clearly.

Then like a thunderbolt the horrible idea of her parents and brother staying in a skyscraper downtown hit her. Now she must refocus her thoughts on finding her own family.

How to get downtown? The horses were panicky and she hadn't even dressed. What to do?

"The house is safe enough for us to re-enter," Robert was talking. "But do not try to go upstairs."

Zelda spoke with all her kindness, "You can borrow some of my clothes. We do have a couple of seasoned horses we can harness."

She is reading my mind. We must go.

CHAPTER 12

Eileen had reached her sister in time to help with the delivery of their healthy baby girl. Carol had been awake and more or less pacing the floor when the earthquake hit and the shaking simply tossed her onto the bed. The quake, while the most devastating one ever to hit San Francisco, had been a little kinder to their area. They had felt the shaking and people more or less rolled with it even though much of their belongings did rattle. While her husband waited in the living room, Carol's midwife stayed with her every moment. Occasionally Joseph would pop his head in the doorway and ask how things were going and would there be anything he could do. Once in a while they sent him to ask the servants for more pillows for his wife's comfort. The midwife had arrived only about ten minutes prior to the quake and spent much of that time trying to persuade Carol to lay down and Joseph to leave the room. The quake settled that dispute. Then she had the added task of calming both parents-to-be as well as the servants. Of course there was damage but it must be put out of everyone's mind so they could concentrate on the moment at hand. It wasn't long before every pillow in the house was forced into service for Carol's comfort.

Labor progressed in a normal fashion but it took a bit longer than anticipated. The distractions seemed to multiply too.

Instead of having an early baby they were busy having a healthy, perfect baby. There was no need for alarm. Carol lay comfortably back in the freshly made bed. The midwife was right. Staying in bed would alleviate most of the panic caused by the earthquake and they could focus on delivery of a healthy baby. It was late in the afternoon while most of San Francisco was weeping with destruction that little Anna Marie entered the world. She was full of optimism and hope for their futures.

"Little but loud," spoke her proud father.

"Anna Marie, meet your Aunt Eileen. She is the one with the bandage on her head," said her tired mother.

"I think you out did us all, Carol. Congratulations to both you proud parents."

The midwife completed her duties and left their stately home. It was obvious to everyone she was concerned for her own family.

"I'll stay until your servants return," said Eileen. "It was kind of you to send them home to locate their families. I so hope for everyone's safety.

"Yes, we do, too. And what a trip it must be for Rita to look for her parents. I wish we had more news about the earthquake. Perhaps it really isn't so bad after all."

"Well, dear we have really been busy waiting for our lovely daughter to be born. We should take advantage of Eileen's kindness and, since you are the mayor's primary advisor, you should go to him. I am certain he would appreciate your presence now no matter how minor or major the earthquake damage is."

"Yes, my line of thinking is the same. I promise I will return at the earliest possible moment. Thank you, Eileen."

As her husband slipped out the door, Carol's eyes became droopy with sleepiness. She soon drifted into a shallow state of sleep with an inner feeling she must remain alert.

When Joseph reached the mayor's office it became obvious to him that this problem would not go away anytime soon. He assumed and remained in a stoic state for a few minutes. Then tears streamed down his face and he finally broke down and sobbed. *How can one day contain so much pleasure and devastation?* He grappled with his inner feelings trying to recapture the soaring excitement he had experienced earlier when his daughter was born. *Wasn't that just a few minutes ago?* He finally offered a prayer of thanks that his family was unharmed. He added an extra few words for their servants then he seemed to babble that all of San Francisco would need help. *Perhaps,* his racing mind thought, *You could even help us restore our fine city.*

Then he calmly walked out of the room and ordered an emergency meeting of the City Planners Commission.

"We are looking at a very long recuperative effort," he said. "It will be our responsibility to assure our citizens of future protection. We will concentrate on convincing everyone of our positive moves towards reconstruction."

And for the second time in her young life, Rita Rodgers sat writing a letter of death. This one was specifically directed to her Aunt Emma in London, England. She tried to soften the words as though she could somehow ease the pain they caused.

My Dearest Aunt Emma,

Perhaps the news has already reached you about our horrific earthquake. Mother and Father were both gone to their final reward by the time I reached them in San Francisco. I am so very grateful we were able to spend a few happy days together before the tragedy struck. With all of the devastation we thought it best to have their funerals performed at the earliest possible convenience.

They are resting together in the local cemetery.

My dearest brother Gary was injured and I, right now, sit in his hospital room sending him my will to live. It is my firm belief that my will permeate his wrecked body and encourage his survival. The doctors, however, have informed me that they hold little hope Gary will ever wake from his coma. They are insisting I care for him in a home environment, which is exactly what I plan to do. There is enough money for me to purchase the boarding house where I live and certainly with its spacious areas I will be able to keep Gary comfortable in a homey atmosphere.

My former landlord, after repairing the home which suffered only minor damage, slipped and fell in a most awkward way as to wrench his back creating a permanently painful condition. He and his lovely wife plan to relocate their living quarters to the San

Francisco waterfront where his brother owns a shipping business. We all pray his painful injury will heal enough to permit him to do paperwork for his brother to keep them afloat. During our horrendous scare everyone was concerned the waterfront may be destroyed, especially by fire. We are fortunate indeed the damage was not ever more severe than our fears.

My purchase of the boarding house is effectual today and I have made arrangements to move Gary home to his own room where he can be afforded the constant care he requires.

I know you are comfortable in London, but if you should decide to experience California we would certainly welcome you into our home. Actually this letter is more a plea to you to award our home with your presence.

With all that's going on around us, I need a trusted Aunt to help me in the day-to-day activities. I know the city will *eventually regain its status as the most cosmopolitan city west of the Mississippi and you could certainly find it a most enjoyable place to live.*

Please consider my request and know you have my love. Warmest thoughts and prayers,

Rita

Rita wired her letter, and with a deep sigh she turned her attention to her brother. With a great deal of care Gary was transported to his new home; a large downstairs bedroom in a boarding house now owned by his sister. Rita spoke to him

constantly during the move but there was not a hint of response. It was kind of Robert and Zelda to stay long enough to prepare Gary's room and see that plenty of food was available for the new owner.

Rita helped see her friends off to their new home on the waterfront. She hoped the pain would lessen quickly and Robert would soon feel better. She knew he would have excellent care with Zelda around and the offer from his brother did sound promising. He had a successful business and plenty of comfortable room for Robert. If the pain ever allowed Robert to move around freely, he would have plenty of paperwork responsibilities to support the business. It was a nice goal for nice people and Rita hoped it would be easily attainable for them.

They were sure to meet again and Rita wanted it to be frequently. She was already looking forward to their friendly compassion.

CHAPTER 13

Rita stood with her Aunt Emma at the gravesite of her brother, Gary.

"We have both lost brothers," whispered Aunt Emma. "Now they rest together."

"Those three graves represent my entire family," Rita was sobbing.

"No, dear. I am your family. We must stay focused and look ahead. While it is so very difficult to lose someone we love, we must realize that the ones who are gone would not want us to dwell on their demise.

We must be grateful for what we had and what we have now. Let's move forward."

Emma had arrived in San Francisco the very day that Gary was diagnosed with pneumonia. He had never regained consciousness from the injury he suffered months ago during the earthquake.

When the doctor left Gary for the last time he said, "Mrs. Rodgers, I am sorry, but it won't be long now." Then after a pause he nodded saying, "It is very nice to meet you, Miss Barnes." Then he quietly left through the front door.

Both ladies sat with Gary not even daring to close their eyes for a moment. It was late the following day that Gary took a deep breath, coughed and slowing stopped living.

"At least he was peaceful," whispered Rita.

Rita had stood and walked across the room and picked up a small satchel. It was soft and she drifted into a trance as she stroked it. *Neither John nor Gary knew what hit them to cause their death. Oh my here it is Autumn and soon it will be Christmas.*

Aunt Emma agreed to stay with her niece indefinitely. She would give it her all to make a good life for them in San Francisco. After all, Emma's specialty was cooking and she had made a fair living with it back in London. Producing her culinary talents for her niece and boarders would be child's play compared to the busy schedule she had left behind in England. There was no apparent reason why she couldn't run

165

this business while Rita concentrated on her efforts towards education. Eileen still lived here and who knows whoever would need a place to live. This house could get very busy indeed. She had confidence she could handle it. Besides, she had seen Rita stroke the small satchel, not with a reflection of her past experiences but rather with a dazed look in her eye that was worrisome. Perhaps, if it continued, she would speak to the doctor about it. He had been so very kind tending to Gary on a regular basis maybe he wouldn't mind addressing another potential problem and...wasn't there something there when he had expressed his pleasure in meeting her? Emma wasn't sure but she decided to wait for Rita's schedule to resume to its high level of demand. Then she could observe her niece and watch for the results.

Time passed slowly at first but, as predicted, busy people tend not to have time for old habits. Those occasions when Rita would sit quietly with her satchel and the far away look in her eyes gradually became less and less frequent.

Emma had no trouble at all becoming immersed in her new life. She reorganized the kitchen and was thrilled when friends requested her breads. Her desserts were a big hit and soon became a valuable source of income for her. Her entrepreneurial spirit soared with excitement. People were even willing to trade their talents for minor repairs around the house just for a few goodies from Emma's kitchen.

Rita, meanwhile, worked with lifted spirits. The idea of having a relative here with her was heartwarming. Especially when that relative was such an excellent cook and so very popular with friends, neighbors and acquaintances.

"It seems strange, Aunt Emma. The way time has passed. Years really and we have never had a real heart to heart."

"I think we have done exceptionally well, Rita. You have such a nice boarding house with such friendly guests. It would be quite enough for one person to own, but you have also incorporated a very important career for yourself."

"Oh, I do feel so gratified. I have pushed so hard to accomplish John and my goals. The school is fantastic. Education for

the primary student in now compulsory and
the length of the school year has surpassed
even my dearest of hopes. Watching these
young minds blossoming into the intellects
this world needs creates an indescribable
feeling. We have made remarkable progress
since I first set foot in San Francisco. And
by the way dear Auntie, this boarding house
is yours too. That was our agreement and it
shall remain that way."

Rita and Emma were casually sitting
at an outdoor table enjoying the sunny
weather and Emma's fine cooking. It was
certainly a welcome respite from the busy
schedules, which had completed another
year of school.

"You know, Rita. With all the
information about Women's Suffrage, I see

nothing odd about you being permitted to purchase a motor car or a horseless carriage. The timesaving and convenience of such a contraption would make it a wise investment indeed. Think of transporting students—and parents, as well—in a fraction of the time it now consumes. It would certainly seem a possibility with your stature as San Francisco's leading school marm."

"I was considering the very same idea, Aunt Emma. Perhaps I should step forward and assert more independence for women. My efforts would represent a mere feather of weight but in time it could help sway people that we should have the right to vote. I realize a ballot in women's hands is in the distant future and a far distant hope."

"Yes, I fear it will not happen anytime soon, but I fear it will never occur if steps are not taken. And you, dear niece, with your position in our society, are the one who needs to help with the baby steps to encourage others."

"I do seem to have reached a lull in my life. I am not complaining, mind you. I truly feel surprised and gratified when I look back at the years gone by. Let's make it a goal to acquire a motorcar as well as the right to safely drive it wherever and whenever we choose. If we cannot accomplish this feat this summer then we will continue working towards that same goal through out the new school year."

"You've got my support. Of course, you do deserve a lull to enjoy a rest. Your constant striving is amazing. Let's approach it calmly and see what issues will evolve. Agreed?"

"Agreed. But only if you support my efforts with more of your superbly tasty treats from your kitchen."

They both broke forth in laughter as they pictured the yummy aromas from the kitchen credited with votes towards Women's Suffrage.

"We have been so fortunate to experience San Francisco. There are reports of Europe being close to war. What a horrible thought and to add to it the possibilities that we could have remained in England and been caught up in the strife. Thankfully our President is not prone to supporting or engaging in any wartime activities. We are safe here in America."

"Yes, Aunt Emma. Woodrow Wilson does seem like a peaceful gentleman. I fear though for the peoples of England and their European neighbors. What are they to do? And don't you and I have a few relatives back there? Oh, I have lost touch."

"There is nothing we can do to aid anyone over there, Rita. As much as we would like to pick them up and deposit them here in our American neighborhood we cannot do more than what we have already offered. We pray for them, but we must work to improve our lives here."

"Aunt Emma, you have described our lives as one great big opportunity. I wish I had spent more time with you at home in

London. All those formative years could have been enriched with your influence."

"We shall take one exciting step after another towards accomplishments together."

CHAPTER 14

War did break out in Europe. Archduke Ferdinand had been assassinated, but America had thus far remained isolated from the strife. Great Britain found herself at war with Germany who was proclaiming all kinds of threatening dangers.

Once again Rita and Emma sat at the kitchen table discussing their safety. Eileen joined them this time and all were frightened.

"Oh, why must we think of war coming to San Francisco? Years ago we experienced a devastating earthquake. That episode in our lives presented quite enough violence for me," commented Eileen to break the silence.

"I arrived only weeks after that horrible experience. I witnessed the deplorable conditions of the aftermath and help tend to my nephew's funeral. He passed on just two days after my arrival. I've been here ever since, building quite a business for my niece and myself. War is something I don't ever want to think about."

Dr. Smith was at the door, anxious to get a taste of Emma's latest baking accomplishment. He, at first, found it an excuse to talk with Emma and soon realized he was truly caring about this family.

"May I join you? I noticed the delicious aroma from your kitchen," Dr. Smith said as he pulled out a chair.

Emma, not sure what to say or do, stood and poured coffee for the four of them. Dr. Smith had spoken with her privately on several occasions, but he always stayed on the subject of Rita. He, too, had noticed the rather eerie behavior when she stroked the small satchel. He told Emma how pleased he was that her own presence was having a positive influence on Rita. He had asked Emma to write in a special book each time she noticed Rita in an action that she considered bizarre. Emma had complied, but over the years these occasions had diminished in frequency. Rita had become overwhelmed with her work, which seemed to boost her energy.

Rita became so enthusiastic and focused at school board meetings it soon became accepted to vote to support her ideas. They had hired dynamite and learned to live the results. Anyway they were pleased with this lady from England and only rarely did they hear a complaint. Rita, at the same time, spent hours preparing some request she knew would benefit the educational system. She knew she would walk away victorious, but she always wanted to be prepared for an argument. One night when Emma had accidentally dropped a tray of baked goods and they had to be replaced for an important event in the neighborhood, Rita had joined in to help bake new ones. Emma had tried to steer Rita to working on a presentation they both knew needed to be ready the following morning, but Rita, ever mindful of what her aunt meant to her, insisted on helping. It was quite late at night when they finally turned in and neither had control over their eyelids. They drooped and no way in the world was Rita going to prepare an in depth presentation for the school board. The next morning, almost without thinking about it, Rita picked up a pile of papers she had previously used for a similar reason. It was an impressive pile of papers and had taken nearly an hour to present. She slipped the papers into her delicate carrying case as she sleepily left her home. The ride to the meeting did nothing to wake her, but to her astonishment the board took one look at her offering and voted unanimously to accept her plea without even hearing it. When she shared this news with Aunt Emma they both giggled and wondered just how far this ploy would take them.

Thereafter whenever Rita had a presentation she would simply outline her request on two pages, but carry twenty more pages to look overwhelmingly involved with time consuming details. And reliving the moment always lightened the conversations around the table with friends.

Now, however, what should have been a pleasant visit with friends with accompanying delicious treats was filled with talk of war.

President Woodrow Wilson had addressed congress asking for a war resolution so America could enter the Great War against imperial Germany.

"Armed neutrality is ineffectual," said Dr. Smith. Then he added, "That comment is a quote from our president, but it explains our situation. We must and we will go to war."

"When John and I wed in London the talk was of doomsday at the turn of the century. It never happened and now here it is 1917 and fears of war are spreading," commented Rita.

"We mustn't take it lightly, Rita. It is definitely a real possibility."

"Oh, Aunt Emma. I know. John was lost in the Spanish American War soon after we arrived here. There is nothing positive about armed conflict. We must be ever mindful of the potential for loss of life. England has been in this war for several years and now we are being drawn into it. Why must we do barbaric battle?"

"Because of imperial Germany. We have strived to remain neutral, but now we must fight for our freedom," Dr. Smith offered.

"Emma, as usual your treats are unbeatable. Best in the world!" Eileen was trying to lighten the mood. The possibility of war was out of their control and Rita was taking it much too personally.

Emma was struggling for words, having been taken aback by Rita's outburst. She had never heard Rita refer to her wedding or the loss of her husband. John was killed nineteen years ago and never once had Rita let anyone know how deeply her pain tugged at her. Emma feared offering support for Dr. Smith and the freedom, which must surely accompany the defeat of the Germans. Yet she was aware that she must not provide Rita with false confidence.

Rita's eyes were afire with a startling look no one had previously seen. They all sat silently frozen to their seats as though the warmth of the freshly baked treats had turned to sticky icy glue that held them in their places.

Dr. Smith ventured another comment, "I am so very impressed with these apricot dandies, Emma. Wherever did you obtain the apricots?"

"Right up the street. Mr. Miller has a few trees in his yard and he provides me with a variety of fruits. Sometimes his kind wife delivers them to me after she sends their children off to school and her husband off to work. She is such a dear and very impressed with our educational system. They truly want Rita to know how very much they appreciate her."

Rita started to soften. She had not heard every word spoken, but a few key words had managed to enter her world. Strong words like...education...school...appreciate.

Eileen caught on and wanted to help. Dr. Smith gave her a sign to commence speaking.

"Rita is always making a presentation to the school board. Been doing that for years. It isn't that she requested anything gigantic that drew attention. It was that genius approach that built up the school system. A lot of little 'Rita Steps' over time have added up to an enormous accomplishment. What an exciting time it was for me to actually see this genius of hers in action. Absolute brilliance."

"Ahhhh. What a relief to experience a depth of inhalation."

Rita had started to relax and automatically followed suit by taking in a deep breath. When she exhaled her tensions eased giving her control over her previous state of fury.

Everyone sat back and relaxed hoping it would be a short war.

Rita excused herself and while walking into her room she grasped her suede satchel, caressing it. "They don't always see everything," she whispered to the emptiness of the room.

CHAPTER 15

Peace. Ahhhhhh sweet peace. The Great War of Wars was nearing an end. America's involvement had helped defeat the Germans just as the President had predicted.

"We shall celebrate!" Rita shouted. "No more war! Ever! Nothing can equal this one."

Emma sat quietly at the table and listened as Rita gave an endless stream of words to proclaim her happiness with peace. Eileen who had had a brief discussion with

Emma joined them after pouring coffee and taking the liberty of offering more tasty treats. She knew what was coming and she feared Rita's reaction.

Rita continued with the excitement, talking and predicting all the vast improvements to San Francisco's educational system. It seemed she never ceased to portray a perfectly schooled society where everyone was learned as well as accomplished at an early age. Yes, Rita had many dreams and was always focused on and reaching for the future she and John had envisioned.

"Rita! Rita!" Emma could no longer contain herself. "I realize your lofty ideals with full understanding, but we have even more devastating news."

Rita sat stunned. *What? How dare her Aunt speak to her like that? What could possibly be more important than education? It must have priority. Isn't that why Aunt Emma is here? To support her efforts to fulfill her and John's dreams?*

"Wh...Wh...What?" she stuttered.

"Dr. Smith has asked for our assistance. The flu."

"Yes, but it is only in pockets somewhere in the world. Spain I heard and in Europe. What on earth could we possibly do about it?" Rita queried.

"Yes it is in Spain and reports are it is deadly. Now it has been noted here in America. Looks like we are in for an epidemic...and it will be worse than the Great War."

"It is rapidly becoming a global disaster. People are dying. If the reports we hear are true the death toll will be in the millions. Apparently a person is either immune to it or dying from it. They talk of four ladies out for an evening of entertainment. Three of them became ill suddenly and they were dead within hours. The fourth is alive and well without experiencing even one symptom. It is difficult to understand, but Dr. Smith needs us to assist him in preparing for the worst," Eileen said in the firmest voice she could muster.

Rita silently sat wondering if she had been babbling all this time. She had been so involved with the tiniest of details in the educational process, that she had let the potential epidemic slip by her. The Great War had taken its toll on Americans including San Francisco residents and Rita had concentrated on not letting it have too much of an impact on the schools. Now, it appeared, another enemy would command the attention of peoples around the globe.

"It's like battling another war," Rita finally spoke but with the softest voice.

"This one is worse, I understand," said Emma in a voice not much stronger than her niece had used.

"Of course you are correct." Rita was speaking as she gathered her thoughts and prioritized them. Then she continued, "I will avail myself in any way possible to squash the fearsome flu...even if it is an enemy we cannot see."

As it turned out the situation rapidly became worse than any nightmare anyone could have imagined.

Rita was the first to suggest the school house be made into a respite for tired workers, but it quickly became a makeshift hospital as ill people swarmed for aid. Cots were hurriedly placed side by side in each room; then tents were added to the playground area surrounding the building itself. The death toll was staggering and it became a matter of struggle to continue with the efforts.

Dr. Smith had taken to staying in Rita's boarding house hoping his presence would dissipate any ideas of annexing it into a part of an emergency hospital. His ploy was effective and the house remained relatively germ free.

"Everyone in the world will either become immune to this illness or die of it," Dr. Smith commented on one of those rare occasions he was afforded a few moments to sit at the table for nourishment.

"All normal life activities have come to a standstill. We are so very fortunate to have acquired the ingredients we need to prepare meals," Emma said.

"Oh, I have heard some people are making a fortune building caskets of all sizes and selling them on street corners. Can you imagine such a horrible undertaking of mercenary efforts?" offered Eileen.

"Your words are ringing like a Grim Reaper's would, Eileen. This epidemic is far worse than the Great War. Certainly the mortality rate is much higher." Rita said in an exhausted tone.

"We must put one foot in front of the other until this horrible mess is done with. It is the only way to think about it," Dr. Smith was giving advice.

"Think? I am much too exhausted to think. It was some time ago I started moving around without so much as a thought as to what I was doing. I have been reliable to the ill only because I am a creature of habit," Rita explained.

"Yes. Your fierce determination you have had inside of you since your early childhood has surfaced once again. This time, however, it has such an ominous tinge around its edges."

"Oh, Aunt Emma. You have always seen more inside of me than anyone. You make me feel as though I am on solid ground as long as I have my determinations to fall back on."

"Yes. I feel that is your finest attribute. At least one of them."

"You are so fortunate. I have ceased to feel anything at all. Now I must get back to work," commented Dr. Smith as he rose from the table. "But not before commending all of you for your outstanding performances during this hideous crisis."

"When it is over...and it will be soon...we can experience a boisterous celebration for the end of the Great War and the defeat of a contagious disease as well." Eileen said in a gallant effort to pump enthusiasm into the atmosphere.

And so they each in their own way adopted the motto: ONE FOOT IN FRONT OF THE OTHER UNTIL WE ARE FINISHED.

They each returned to their routine. Dr. Smith walked among the ill, too often calling for another casket. At the same time he would help clear airways so patients could inhale life sustaining air. He felt inadequate knowing the flu would take these people soon despite his efforts. He also noted the ones who obviously had pneumonia and made a mental note to check them again later. They would be dead within hours and he wanted the cadavers removed immediately. He wished for more efficiency, but realized he was fortunate to have any procedure at all.

Meanwhile many of the well people spent their time sponging the ill and helping to maintain airways. People were dying while struggling for air with many gushing bloody froth from their mouths and nostrils prior to suffocating.

As Eileen leaned to sponge a newcomer's forehead she caught the hem of her dress on the corner of his cot. The dress ripped as it tugged just enough to throw her off balance and she fell across the mid section of the very person she was trying to help.

"No worry, ma'am." He could barely speak. "So grateful for your attendance."

Eileen began to weep openly as she made her way out of the tent. She stumbled once, but then quickly regained her balance. Then as she stepped outside in the fresh air she collapsed. Eileen was dead within hours and her body became lost in a sea of caskets.

The solemn atmosphere of her passing was not lost. Everyone regained a spirit of momentum to conquer this dastardly illness.

CHAPTER 16

It was late...very late. Rita and Emma sat at the kitchen table.

"I'll make us some fresh coffee, but we will have to be satisfied with yesterday's treats."

"Sounds good to me. We can simply expand our celebration. What a dramatic change for our lives. The flu epidemic stopped as abruptly as it started. Further women are now allowed to vote and are we ever enjoying the roaring twenties."

"It hurts so that Eileen isn't here. I can still hear her laughter at our table. She was the one who always tried to pump optimism into everyone she met."

"And she had plans for the biggest celebration in history."

"And it is still so difficult to accept the death of President Harding. To think he died right here in San Francisco! Dr. Smith was in attendance but of course he cannot share information with us. We are left to wonder if our president died as they say of a heart attack or was assassinated. There is even talk of suicide. What dreadful possibilities, but it will remain mysterious for the duration of history. A heart attack is probable, but after only two years as our president it does feel uncomfortable to simply accept what they are saying."

"Well, we mustn't pressure Dr. Smith. He is bound by duty not to discuss any details that may have come to his attention. Even though we worked so closely with him during that horrible flu epidemic."

"Oh, it was horrible. I still miss Eileen. I do wish she were here to celebrate with us. And to vote. I do believe she would be the one person who would truly enjoy living in today's society. No doubt, she would be a live wire. Maybe even a flapper at a speakeasy."

They both giggled knowing they would never talk about a friend except in kindness and loving terms.

"I can hear her laughing at Eddie Cantor and see her bouncing to the music of Al Jolson. Oh, hate that dratted flu for taking her."

Emma tried to change the subject, "Isn't air travel just astonishing? Charles Lindberg may fly around the world next. Already planes are flying mail from coast to coast in America—they have practically obliterated the trains."

Rita paused remembering her own cross-country trip in her own Pullman car. It had afforded her a peaceful and restful experience at a time when she most needed it. *Indeed,* she thought, *no airplane will ever replace that.*

"Well, we could go on and on about bootleggers, Al Capone, flappers and what have you, but the truth is I must travel to town to purchase staples. If I don't there will be no baked goods for tomorrow. I do hope you will travel with me."

"Yes, I think it will be great fun shopping together. It has simply been ages since you and I have had a lark of some kind. Let's do up these few things and be off to town early in the morning. I do so want to visit that new bookstore I have heard so much about."

The single most liberating invention in the world was the automobile and it became very popular in the 1920s. The Model T was Henry Ford's answer to transporting the masses and since it was mass-produced it was relatively inexpensive.

As Emma and Rita climbed into their Model T and started off on their jaunt to town Emma shouted, "HENRY FORD FOR PRESIDENT!"

Rita had not even an inkling her aunt could explode with such joyous excitement. She joined in with laughter and they both became so elated they could hardly contain themselves on the way to town.

Everything became funny. Tears were streaming down their faces as Rita finally brought the car to a halt. They both bounced out looking forward to their respective shopping places.

"I'll return to the car with the much needed supplies and if you aren't here I will look for you in the book store." Emma said while she yet giggled.

"Oh, Aunt Emma. I love you. I am so very pleased we can be together to experience this wonderful new era."

"I love you too, Rita. My favorite niece in the whole world. Wouldn't change a thing." Emma waved as she crossed the street.

Rita sauntered about a half a block and slipped into the new bookstore.

Rita was hoping to find a book about the race riots in Tulsa in 1921. She wanted to learn every detail and planned to write an essay to present to students. It would be a learning experience for them and a good addition to their library. But search as she might there was not a shred of information in book form. There were copies of news articles but she had already pored over them to a point of obsession.

The literary modernism displayed in books had originated in Paris. All of the young writers were spending as much time as they could in that City of Wonderment. Rita was interested in securing books by James Joyce and Arthur Conan Doyle. She herself didn't care for horror stories and mysteries, but it was amazing how ladies of the community were flocking to the library. Ever since the ladies were afforded the right to drive cars they found themselves with extra time on their hands. Their errands were accomplished with such efficiency they were now broadening their lives with more reading material and furthering their education. Some were even accepting part-time jobs and they surely would appreciate a good book during restful moments.

Of course she would also need books by Ernest Hemmingway. His writing always generated conversation. Rita had offered the schoolhouse for book discussion meetings and some of them got rather lively. A comment or two about Hemmingway's style of writing would generally quiet a room.

Gertrude Stein was another important purchase of the day. She had a unique way of capturing people's attention whether they liked it or not. The Making of Americans was the most popular choice of her writing and when she said 'A rose is a rose is a rose is a rose is a rose...' the discussions tended to last well into the evening.

People were soon quoting Gertrude Stein whenever there seemed to be no obvious answer to a posed question. It became laughable and Rita thought any lightheartedness would enhance the learning process. It became especially true when children saw it in adults.

"Ezra Pound. Ahhh now there is a poet. Have to have poetry to support our library. Even though Ezra Pound was an unconditional supporter of James Joyce, his writings are valuable," whispered Rita to no one as she fingered one of his books.

"Pardon me? May I be of any assistance? I am the proprietor of this store. Indeed if there is perhaps something special you'll be seeking please know we are able to order it."

"Thank y…"

The door crashed open with an excited gentleman shouting, "An accident. Oh my God. An accident."

Whatever could he be referring to? thought Rita. Then after a pause, "Has someone fallen? The sidewalk was a bit slippery from a recent rain, but anyone using care should not have suffered a fall."

"What is it, sir? What is it?" asked the proprietor.

Rita thought she hadn't even had a chance to introduce herself to this gentleman and she so wanted to meet the person who envisioned this new bookstore.

"A lady," the breathless man continued. "She was carrying a few bags across the street and a Model T came along

209

and slammed right into her. She muttered something about this bookstore. We don't know what it means."

Rita turned pale and books slipped from her hands falling to the floor. Her knees started to buckle but the two gentlemen hoisted her. Then she insisted she be led out the door to see this accident.

Dr. Smith was in attendance stooping over a person in the middle of the muddy road. Bought items were scattered in the immediate area.

"I'm sorry, Rita," he said as he took both her hands. "Emma is gone."

CHAPTER 17

Following the funeral of Emma Barnes, Rita sat at the kitchen table sipping tea with a few friends. She was unaware Dr. Smith had slipped a sedative into her drink. She heard herself repeating the words, "...this table was so very lonely without Eileen and now without Emma it will be devastatingly bare..."

Emma had been laid to rest beside her brother and his wife. Her nephew, Gary, rested next to his mother.

"She is part of everything in this house," Rita muttered.

"You have lots of friends. We are all here to help you. All of us will miss Emma immensely but we have an idea that will keep her memory with us forever. We would like to produce a cookbook containing her fabulous recipes. It seems she always made off-the-cuff comments when asked about her baking. Like 'Oh, I use more sugar...' or 'I cook them to near gelatin stage before adding them to...' Don't you see, Rita? All of us would like to hold regular meetings and try to correlate all of these comments into a recipe book," Mrs. Miller was speaking since she felt closer to Emma having supplied her with fruits.   Besides the Millers lived only two doors away.

"I understand," said Rita.   "Each person will supply snatches of information about a recipe and we are to put them together in a most delicious way."

"Yes.   The memory of her delicious desserts will live forever, but the bits of information on how they were prepared may fade."

"We can have the meetings at the school.   Perhaps we should initiate them on the morrow."

"I'll take care of it," offered Mrs. Miller.   "I'll contact as many people as I can. We shall meet in Emma's name."

Rita slowly moved her eyes towards Dr. Smith. They were droopy and she could no longer deny her drowsy state. She quietly slipped into her room and immediately became engulfed in the warmest deepest sleep she had experienced for years.

When she awoke her thoughts were of her aunt describing her as such a determined person even during her childhood.

"Oh, Emma," she whispered. "Life was so much easier with you here...and a lot more jovial." Rita was remembering their last moments together laughing like silly schoolgirls but at the same time she was quietly stroking the soft satchel with Christmas ornaments inside.

Rita collected herself and calmly stepped forward into the life she was expected to live.

Mrs. Miller chose to address the group. They had been meeting at the schoolhouse for quite a long time in an attempt to secure a good cookbook from fragments of information from Emma.

"What are we to do? We must disband and be off our own ways. We've seen far too many tangents and the waters are murkier than ever," she said in exasperation.

"I want to hear from Rita," someone spoke and support for the suggestion rang from the roomful of people.

Rita stepped forward welcoming the chance to speak casually to friends rather than seriously to the school board.

"We have all been hazy of late. Life has handed us a depression and we will deal with its devastations. We will prevail of course. The run on the banks; unemployment skyrocketing; and Wall Street woes.

"There are many people in need and here is my suggestion. We can meet once a month at my place...where the baking started. As you know I, myself, have accepted two needy families into my home and they have aided immensely with chores and duties. Since all of us are on the severest of restrictions for obtaining ingredients we will share what we have. It is very difficult to obtain butter but one of us can supply one pound a month. If done on a rotating basis no one will miss it...hardly. Also, on a rotating basis, one person can donate their share of chocolate. Each month the shared ingredients will be processed to the best of our memories and hopefully reproduce Aunt Emma's desserts. When we are all satisfied with the recipe it will be printed in its final form and archived for future correlation.

"We can also use the time to chat about the news and pray for a speedy recovery from this depression. And, hopefully, it will give each of you an incentive to reach out to the needy."

"It's a good idea. It's smart. None of us has any money right now and what Rita is proposing will provide enlightenment and a sense of doing. After all there is absolutely no hurry to accomplish a book. Rather we can plan an enjoyable time once a month. I support Rita's suggestion. It sounds like a delightful break in our depressed state," Mrs. Miller spoke.

So it was done. The meetings, soon dubbed the 'Yummy Meets', were held without stress or concern for anything except a recipe. Each month different people were expected to provide a part of the baking ingredients. The final product, of course, was divided among everyone to take home to test on their families. All were pleased for there were also good conversations and good friendships developing. There was always talk of the new president Franklin D. Roosevelt and his New Deal. There was worrisome talk of a man called Adolf Hitler in Germany and other political extremisms as well. But the meetings were always informative and thought provoking. Everyone began looking forward to the next meeting and people started paying closer attention to the news so they, too, could contribute to the conversations.

Secretly Rita thought *Emma would be so pleased with the excitement these meetings have generated. I wouldn't put it past her to deliberately leave us with a conundrum for this very reason.* Then she mentally pictured Aunt Emma smiling.

The depression was moving agonizingly slow. No one could predict its end and few people understood what initiated it. They knew it started in America and began with the New York Stock Market crash in 1929. By 1933 eleven thousand banks had failed. There had been twenty-five thousand banks considered reliable but now if any money at all was available people hid it in their own homes. Hiding ideas flourished and one in particular caught the fancy of many as they dug up their dirt basements to bury their treasures.

Unemployment was pushing thirty per cent and families broke apart as men traveled to find work. Meager amounts of food were served to the hungry as soup lines appeared.

The financial collapse of America led to the financial collapse of other countries as well. Adolf Hitler was gaining momentum in Germany and F. D. Roosevelt continued to be elected President of the United States.

"It's touchy at best. Europe is on the brink of war again," Dr. Smith said to Rita on one of those rare occasions when they could chat for a few minutes.

They sat at the kitchen table with coffee and a few treats.

Rita mused, "This table has a history all its own. I am so happy I didn't let it go for a new one like Emma wanted before she died. It has stood remarkably well through an earthquake, The Great War, a bacterial epidemic and a Great Depression. How much more can we ask of it? Another war in Europe? At least this one shouldn't affect us. The table is telling us we are safe.

Whenever we had our talks at this table I felt safe."

"We don't know what is happening in Europe. However, my dearest Rita, you are right. We must keep our thoughts on our own lives. It was so nice of you to take in two needy families. I fear they may have starved if it weren't for you."

"Oh, quite the contrary. It was they who rescued me. Not only did they keep up with repairs and regular chores, the two men had one gun between them and would hunt for food. Goodness, we have consumed a variety. Rabbits, birds and even venison has gotten us through the roughest of times."

"Well. It seems to be letting up now. The depression I mean. People are starting to secure jobs and return to their families. Banks are reopening with insurance and even some doctors are being called back to work in hospitals. There are major efforts being made to avoid such a disaster in the future. Ten years is a long time to fight back but we made it."

"Yes. One foot in front of the other," Rita said distantly.

"With a new decade upon us we should think optimistically. The forties have to be an improvement. We are safe and we go on."

"I agree," avowed Rita. "And I have been saving something just for this occasion. Join me in a drink?"

Rita uncovered a bottle of Canadian Club Whiskey and prepared to partake.

"Rita the Rascal! You've been hiding that all this time!" Dr. Smith was secretly pleased.

CHAPTER 18

Rita awoke early to prepare for church services. Although clothing styles had changed over the years making life easier for women, her body had aged. So she moved a bit slower with some creakiness here and there. A touch on her hair do was sufficient since it was rarely mussed. The radio played softly as she prepared her breakfast and completed her attire. Everyone else in the boarding house chose to sleep in today.

Rita enjoyed her few quiet moments alone and picked up her soft satchel to stroke it. She remembered a framed picture of Aunt Emma and placed it inside the satchel with the homemade Christmas ornaments. It seemed appropriate. She sat on a chair by the table stroking the satchel with a far away look in her eye.

The abrupt interruption that aborted her serene state tore at her like a saber slicing into her very being. So profound was her pain that she barely heard the news and then only key words.

The radio blared with the news "...announcement...We are at war...Japanese war planes have attacked Pearl Harbor...attack continues...urging everyone to stay home...inside..."

"No. Not this time," whispered Rita. She calmly walked to her car and drove. She did not even think of church or school. She simply drove.

Japan? And how she had worked to save pearls for her wedding. It simply won't be tolerated. She would have to tell them.

She drove aimlessly barely taking note of bumps and hills and other drivers. It was dangerous the way she swerved her car. Finally she was forced to park her car after she felt a terrific pang travel through her body. The pain had shot through her spine then eased a bit so she could gather her thoughts. She was parked at the beach with the Pacific Ocean in front of her. The precious satchel lay beside her on the seat. She held it close to her as she stepped from the car and walked towards the coastal waters. As she stepped into the cold ocean Rita began to shout, "NOT THIS TIME...NO MORE WAR...I WILL STOP THIS RIGHT NOW."

When she was waist deep she opened the satchel and pulled out an item that felt soft and filled her entire hand.

"I HAVE A BOMB HERE...I WILL MAKE YOU UNDERSTAND...THERE WILL BE PEACE FOR US."

With all of her strength she threw the ornament as far as she could in the direction of Japan. "I HAVE MORE BOMBS TO STOP YOU..."

The water of the Ocean of the Pacific became chest deep and she mustered all of

her remaining strength to throw the rest of
the items.

"I WILL SWIM THE REST OF THE
WAY TO SHOW YOU...I WILL PROVE
TO YOU...NO MORE WAR..."

CHAPTER 19

The day after the attack on Pearl Harbor, Mrs. Rice was more than a little concerned. People were near panic and the schools were closed. She had promised her own two children and three of their friends an outing and they had settled on a brief outing at the beach. Mrs. Rice had secretly hoped it would tucker the children, preparing them for a long nap after consuming a hot meal. She sighed with relief when she saw the heavy dense fog from last night had lifted and the children were truly enjoying the beach. It did seem to be the safest place for an outing.

"Mrs. Rice! Mrs. Rice! Look what we found! They look like old Christmas ornaments! Billy found one with writing on it."

Anxious to display his reading talents in front of his friends, Billy held the soggy item and read aloud, "'John and Rita Rodgers 1897'"

"Who are they Mrs. Rice?"

END

ABOUT THE AUTHOR

Lila Tanabe is scientifically published and accustomed to doing thorough research. She has also retained her intense interests in historical events. Further she is familiar with the unique world of competition, having won two National Championships in a sport. She also authors the FYI at her workplace.

www.ingramcontent.com/pod-product-compliance
Lightning Source LLC
Chambersburg PA
CBHW022246290526
45785CB00015B/250